Dear
Companion

The Civil War Letters
of
Silas I. Shearer

*For Spencer Conquero's
Teacher —
With Best Regards.
Harold D. Brinkman
april 27, 2008*

Edited and Published
by
Harold D. Brinkman

© 1995 First Printing
Second Printing, 1996

Sigler Printing & Publishing, Inc.
Ames, Iowa 50010-0887

Library of Congress Catalog Card Number: 95-90416
ISBN Number 0-9635812-9-5

For
Kimberley Sue and Susan Kay
Great, Great, Grandaughters
of
Silas and Jane

With Love

Lord only knowes how soon he might of been a priseoner or under the sod by the Rebles ball.

Silas I. Shearer
23rd Iowa Volunteers

Silas I. and Elizabeth Jane Shearer

Introduction

The letters of Silas Shearer were kept in a Black Tin Box in the attic of Minnie Shearer Kimberley, who was one of 11 children of Silas and Jane Shearer. Minnie was my Grandmother and lived next door to me in Colo, Iowa while I was growing up. I am the son of Mildred Jane Kimberley Brinkman who was a daughter of Minnie and John B. Kimberley which makes me a Great Grandson of Silas and Elizabeth Jane Shearer.

While I was growing up another daughter of Silas and Jane lived with us. This would be Catherine LuAnna Shearer Diggins, better known as Aunt Kate. Oh what I would give if they both were still alive and I could talk with them about Silas and Jane.

As you read the letters you will realize the emotions of the Civil War Period. Happiness, Sadness, Worry, Anger, Hope, Frustration, to name a few. A poignant letter from Silas's Mother, Catherine, lamenting the fact that she had 2 sons killed, 2 sons missing, and only Silas, as far as she knew, still alive.

I was aware of the Black Tin Box for a long time. Ruth Kimberley Goodenow, who lived with my Grandmother Minnie during her later years talked about them occasionally. It wasn't until I stopped at the site of Andersonville Prison in Southern Georgia and found the names of Andrew Shearer and Elias Shearer, the missing brothers of Silas, in the Civil War Records of the Prison, that my interest really peaked. Andrew and Elias were able to survive the miserable conditions of Andersonville and both returned home in the Summer of 1865. This was in the Spring of 1989. Upon my return home I asked Aunt Ruth about the letters and she gave them to me along with the Tin Box. There are approximately 130 letters most still in the original envelope many with the 3 cent stamp still affixed. Most were addressed to Elizabeth Jane at Edenville, Marshall County, Iowa. Edenville is now known as Rhodes, Iowa but the cemetery there is still called the Edenville Cemetery.

The letters are in beautiful condition for being 130 years old but a few of the letters are faded and hard to read. Silas, however, had a very good hand but was not much for punctuation. Nor did he always use the correct spelling that we use today. Some of the words were written as they sounded to him and there were some words I just couldn't make out. I was able to follow along pretty well after I became use to his style of writing. *(A photo copy of a letter is included.)*

You will find many references to historical fact. The re-election of Abraham Lincoln over General George McClellon, the battles of Vicksburg and Mobile Bay, are examples. Going on a little spree Christmas Day and then confessing to Elizabeth Jane before she heard it from someone else, executing a traitor are other interesting antidotes. You will find his opening lines are practically all the same. One thing you will definitely realize is Silas was a very strong person and did not take kindly to having his actions and thoughts questioned.

Since I started working on this book we have traveled to Civil War Battlefields including Gettysburg where the most horrible battle of the entire War was fought along with Vicksburg and Mobile Bay where Silas fought the Rebs. At Vicksburg I had a nice visit with the Park Historian. We found Silas mentioned in several records having to do with the Vicksburg Battle along with the monument of the 23rd Iowa Volunteers. I also found where Simeon was buried. Simeon was Silas's brother who was fatally wounded and died March 25, 1862. Silas refers to this in several of his letters. Simeon sent several letters back home and I have included them in the beginning of the letters. He is buried in the Mound City U. S. Military Cemetery located outside of Cairo, Illinois.

Three years ago I was able to visit with John Sellers, who is in charge of the Civil War Section of the Library of Congress. He was amazed at the condition and number of letters and agreed with me that they should be published into book form. It was at this time that he took me through three locked doors into this big room full of Library Stacks. We were in the Library of the Presidents. Here are kept the writings of all the Presidents since George Washington. I held the Diary of George Washington. I read letters written by Thomas Jefferson and Abraham Lincoln. This area is not opened to the public but is reserved for researchers or others having a need for this information. Janet and Kim were with me and we felt indeed honored to be able to view this part of our American History.

Mr. Sellers stated that the Library would like to have the letters to have for their permanent collection. Mr. James H. Billington, Librarian of Congress has also provided access to having this book placed in the Library.

Mr. Billington and Mr. Sellers said the Library of Congress would guarantee the safety of the collection for at least 500 years and they would be made available to researchers and scholars of the Civil War period. Some time in the future, I will give these original letters to the Library of Congress.

We begin with early letters before the war. They explain the hardships of that time.

I hope you enjoy reading these letters. I certainly have enjoyed putting them together. Its just amazing that we are able to follow the Civil War life of our Great Grandfather 130 years after the fact. He was a brave man. It was a very horrible War. I just wish I had had the opportunity to know him personally although I feel I know him through his letters.

Due to lack of punctuation some of the sentences may not make sense during the first reading. Jean Heintz of Heintz's Computer Creations of Nevada, was very helpful with the layout which made the letters easier to understand. I corrected very little for punctuation so you may have to re-read several times. Some are boring, some are really funny, some makes you want to cry, but I am just thankful that his legacy was left for all those who carry the Blood of this Brave Civil War Veteran and his Brave Pioneer Wife.

Harold Brinkman, Great Grandson,
760 14th Street Place
Nevada, Iowa 50201

April 1995

Camp near West Plane Mo.
February the 7th 1863

Dear Companion

it is again I write you a few to let you
know that I am in tolerable good health
and the boys are principly well I hope
these lines will find you all enjoying good
health I received from you dated January
the 4th it came to me the first inst and
yesterday I received three more dated
January the 12th 15th and 18th and I was
glad to hear that you was all well such
letters as that pleases me as long as I can heare
of you enjoying good health I can be sadisfied
Nelson is at Ironton Hospital and that
was the last I heard from him I do not know
how he is geting a long if you hear from
him I want you to write to me and let
me know how he is for I am a good ways
from him I wisht he was heare he could
get to go home I think with out a doubt

4

Silas Shearer

Silas Shearer was born in 1838 in Indiana. His folks along with two other families left by covered wagon in 1847 and settled in Wapello County Iowa. He learned the trade of wagon maker in Jefferson County. He came to Des Moines in 1856 and in November of that same year he left for Nevada in Story County. D. J. Norris overtook him and brought him on in to Nevada where he stayed in the Log Cabin Hotel known as the "Old Terrific". He left the following morning by foot with grip in hand for the SE part of Story County where he had two uncles. On the way he later said he passed through the most God forsaken country that ever was, now one of the best.

In 1862 he enlisted in Co. K 23 Iowa Volunteers. The recruiter came by and he just left with him with barely enough time for a good-by to Jane. He was discharged in 1865 coming out of the Army as a Sergeant. When he went in there were 1070 members of the 23rd Iowa Volunteers and 316 remaining when he was mustered out.

He was an Assessor, Justice of the Peace, on the Board of Story County Supervisors when the second Courthouse was built. His name is listed seven times in Allen's History of Story County. His son-in-law John B. Kimberley said Silas was the most honest man that he ever knew.

Jane Shearer came in the Spring of 1856. They came by rail and steamboat to Kansas City to settle in the New Territory. Drought and the Slavery issue made her parents change their mind, so they bought a wagon and team and moved to a place called Edenville near Rhodes, Iowa. Jane's father Benjamin Shenkle bought 200 acres of timber and prairie land in southeast Story County.

Michael Shearer and Catherine McCord
Michael Shearer was born October 17, 1799 in Maryland
Catherine McCord was born May 7, 1817 in Ohio
They were married May 30, 1835
To this union Silas I. Shearer was born January 11, 1838 in Indiana

Benjamin Shenkle and Edith Day
Benjamin Shenkle was born November 28, 1814 in Ohio
Edith Day was born June 1, 1815 in Ohio
They were married May 15, 1835
To this union Elizabeth Jane Shenkle was born October 6, 1840 in Indiana.

Silas I. Shearer and Elizabeth Jane Shenkle

Silas I. Shearer and Elizabeth Jane Shenkle were married November 30, 1859.
To this union were born:
Lewis Denver Shearer, October 17, 1860
Eliza Ellen Shearer, October 9, 1862
Benjamin Ransom Shearer, May 21, 1866
John Sanford Anderson Shearer, January 5, 1868
Willie J. Shearer, August 17, 1869
Minnie Matilda Shearer, August 10, 1870
Orrie Belle Shearer, August 16, 1872
Catherine LuAnna Shearer, June 21, 1874
Elias Walter Shearer, August 21, 1876
Hattie S. Shearer, April 21, 1879
James Garfield Shearer, October 14, 1881

The marriages of the Shearer children were as follows:

Denver Shearer and Lillie Oxmun, December 24, 1885
Ella Shearer and Lewis Bence, May 10, 1880
Sanford Shearer and Florence Cline, January 1, 1890
Minnie Shearer and John B. Kimberley, March 21, 1891
Orrie Shearer and W. C. Heintz, May 14, 1889
Catherine Shearer and E. L. (Pete) Diggins, November 24, 1894
Walter Shearer and Anna Etnire, October 27, 1897
Hattie Shearer and Allie Girton, September 17, 1896
James Garfield Shearer and Ollie Robinson, February 10, 1903

Willie J. Shearer died at Birth, August 17, 1869
Benjamin Ransom Shearer died January 12, 1908 - age 42

Elizabeth Jane Shearer died February 20, 1914 - age 73
Silas I. Shearer died March 5, 1915 - age 77

They are buried in the Evergreen Cemetery, Collins, Iowa

August the 14th AD 1847

1 Dear Brother I take my pen in hand to inform you that I am well and the rest of
the folks are well. I will be pleased if these few lines will find you injoying good

Health and Uncle Wesley all well so endeth the Chapter

2 I have worked 16 days in the harvest field at the Price of $1.20 cts per day ther was six of us bound and two shocked Wheat and kept up with the Mcvey & Slaters Reaping machine. They cut 170 acres and finished the 13th of this month So ends the Chapter

3 The Measels is rageing down here two of Uncle Pettys girls have the Measels and many others that I will not name there stop now

4 LoDaniel Pools wife is nearly Blind with some other disease With it and Daniel offers every Bit of his property for sale that is a House and two lots and one milk cow and all of his house furniture in abingdon for I like money.

Robert Hayes & family Henry Cougen & wife & son Gus Cougen & family John Silvers & family George Couger & family David Cougen & family all in one crowd started to Kansas and John Hayse Bill Whealer & family went to Kansas

Silas Come down here for the folks all want to see you.
Mother sayes you can go Back if you want to
So no more Simeon Shearer to Silas I Shearer
excuse my bad writing

addressed to Silas I Shearer - Newton Post Office - Jasper County Iowa

April the 30th A D 1856

Dear Brother I take this Opetunity to inform you that we are all well at present and we hope that these few lines may find you well We would like to hear from you, the folks wants to hear from you Silas Write and let us know how you and your Boys gets along there was a Protacted meeting at the meeting house they got 11 joiners Staff Couger was at the mourner bench there is school here now A School Miss from Britan Ameala Dunavan the old miss is gone D Shearer M Dunavan C Mcbeech All of britan they are a going to put Stem works to it They have the Well dug now The price is one hundred and 75 dollars for the out side works nothing in the Shed the Shed alone for $30 dollars The folks would like to see you Silas I would like to see you to One week after you left here the Colt was feet first

J Mcguir wife is not expected to live She has the consumption Silas ask Elick

Troxel if he can cure the hole evel by a Charm if he can send a letter up if you please Mother would like to see you or hear from you rite soon Mr. Troxel lives in Fairfield go as quick as you can for tom is worse that he was

 We have our fens about done We have twenty acres of the best Wheat there is any place around

Uncle Robert has sold his farm how much did he get 17 hundred dollars to I Slater

Send up and lets us know how you and the trade agrees Corn up if you can

So no more at present Rite Sil or Dye

From Simeon Shearer to Silas I. Shearer

This is a letter written by Richard McCord who is a first cousin to Silas Shearer. *Silas's mother was a McCord.*

Hancock County
State of Indiana
June the 18th A. D. 1857

Dear Cousin:

I received your letter this instant and was glad to hear that you were well and the rest of the Connection. I am in tolerable good health and the remainder of the family are the same. Times are hard here, but it appears they are not so hard here as in Iowa from the receipt of your letter. Price of produce wheat $1.50 per bushel, Corn $0.75 per bushel, Meat 10 cts - 12 cts per pound. Wheat looks tolerable well but it is going to be very late before it is ready to be cut. It is just coming out in head. Their is a fair prospect of Oats. Corn looks pretty slim on account of wet weather and needs plughing very much.

More about the Gals!!!!!!!!!!!!!!!!!!
I am very sorry to hear that the girls are so scarce in Marshall County probably they will be plenty after a little while. But as you and Edward sent your respects to girls I will pop the question in favor of you two, and if I received a favorable answer, I will send you word: wherein I think there will be no denial for there are plenty here. But the right kind are hard to get on the right side, off. I expect I'd best quit writing about the girls, for I see I am getting excited and make a great many mistakes, which makes my wrighing appear vulgar.

More about the gals continued ...

you spoke of the girls being so wild that you could not get in less than a hundred yards of them and they went with their heads and tails up. In reply to this I would say let their heads be so and their tails more so. I think probably their heads and tails will come down whenever the sighns come right. My ink is very poor and my pen gathers lint; so I expect I'd best fetch my letter to a close for fear I make a few more mistakes. Write soon, sooner the better.

Yours respectfully,

Richard McCord

Many scroll drawn on the bottom of this letter along with the word PENMAN-SHIP in nice sweeping lines.

"BRIDGE WATER"

Near to Bridge water a rich man lived
Who had two Sons and one Daughter fair
From life to death he was bereaved
To fill his childrens hearts with care
Now to the Sea those two boys ventured
For to bring home their Fathers gain
And an apprentice bound by a firm Indenture
All for to cross the raging main

This young man was of a fair complexion
Was neat and handsome in every limb
On him their Sister placed her affection
But unbeknown to any of them
Excepting two of her youngest Brothers
Who chanced to see them Sort and Play
He told the secret unto no other
But to his Brother he this did say

Perhaps s he is of some poorer family
And thinks he will our Sister have
But will soon put an end to all their Courtship
And quickly send him to his Grave
Now to begin this cruel Slaughter
And to bring on their Sister's woe
This young man they did care and fatten
A game of Hunting for to go

It was in a Woods that was unfrequented
Where harmless birds did sport and play
These two bloody villians was contented
until they took his sweet life away
It hapened near a surface of water
Where the green briars thick did grow
And for to hide this evil slaughter
This young man they did Kill and Throw

When they came home their Sister asked them
What have you done with your Servent man
She says the reason it seems to whisper

Could tell me Brothers if you can
We lost him in a game of hunting
And never more we could him see
We tell you plainly we were offended
And why need you discontented be

That very night as she lie sleeping
She dreamed her true love came and stood
At her bedside in tears Conienting
Appearing in one gore of Blood
He says my dear and most aemiliest Jewel
Tis a folly for you to pine

Since your two brothers has been so cruel
In such a place you may me find
So very early the next morning
She walked alone alone alone
Until she came to this surface of water
And there she found him killed and thrown
The blood on his pale cheeks was dryed
And tears as salt as any brine
She kissed over and then times over
Sayeing Oh; this bosom friend of mine

She stayed there three days and three nights weeping
all alone alone alone alone
When she went home her Brothers asked her
What made her look so pale and worn
She says the reason you've acted Treason
And you have killed your servant man

Now you do think I will hide his murder
But I will do no such thing
Since you have robbed me of my Jewell
Now for his sake you both shall sorry
Now both of them confined in prison
And both of them condemed to die
And for his sake she is lamenting
And yielding up herself to Die

For a friend   Silas Shearer
Written probably 1858 by the paper used

August the 22nd A.D. 1857

(Letter badly faded)

Dear brother it is with the greatest of pleasure that I Embrace myself to inform you that I am well and the rest of the friends are all well as far as I know We received a letter from you dated August the 4th and you said that you was in the heart of the harvest & so we was in the heart of the harvest too Crops looks fine for in some places if they was much finer there would'ent Be any thing of them and hope that these lines may you and the rest of the friends in good health. I expect that there will be some person out of this neighborhood up there this Fall Uncle Andy and Mother talks of going up there in the coarse of Three or Four weeks We have some grass to cut and ten or thirty five acres to break and I dont know which I guess likely I will come up there this Fall

You wrote that you owned four lots in Defience and that you was a going to build a store room this fall Dogonyou I know what sort of a house it is, You think you will get married Well you do now thats what I am comeing up there for to see your store room when you get her if you please

Now you would like to know how I took the hint so quick; As Dock Mcvey says anybody can take the hint when he gets kicked out of doors We call by Gut Uncle Wesley must have been a giveing you another quarter to go to see about that more room of yours or you would not have went to see her Well now he did so he did

Mother thinks you are a big ox cause you dont come down
So no more but remains your affectionate brother.
I wrote to you the 14th of August so I did
Direct your letters to Competine if you please
There is no tax on your lot as I know of
Charles MCullock is married Tell the Esquire to write
All jokes free in harvest so no more
Simeon S. Shearer to Silas I. Shearer

(Letter is folded into an envelope and stamped with 3 cent paid to Silas I. Shearer Newton IA Post Office Jasper Co - Competine Iowa August 28, 1857)

12

Wapello Co Iowa
Jan 2nd 58

Dear Brother and Sister With much pleasure I this pleasant evening will try and write you a few lines. Yours which I received some days since found us all well and I hope this may find you all well I am going to School this winter. Although I do not go regular enough to learn much We have a good Teacher and I like to go very well. I have went fifteen days and am over half way through the Arithmetic I want to get through the Arithmetic and I think I will as I expect to go all the after this week as I have now got a place to keep my horses It will take me two or three more days to fix a place and get us some corn that I have bought. I paid twenty five cts per bushel for corn My team cost me two hundred and fifty five dollars, and thirty five dollars for a set of harness. Artensas and myself has rented a place between us There is 80 acres mostly all in cultivation. We give a third for the use of the place one year. I expect you know where the place is, it is the place that Leveretto Williams use to own Slater now owns it. By the time I buy a wagon my outfit will cost as much or more than yours did. It depends on what kind of a wagon I buy. I did think I would buy a new one out of the Shop but they are to high at the present but are comeing at a lower price than sometime back. I thought I would tend to my ground next year mostly all corn in the fall sell it and go to Missouri and lay all my money that I will have left at that time in land. I have some notion of going there this winter but finaly come to the conclusion to go to school as I still in need of more Schooling, and I think will in the long run pay me better than if I went to Missouri

I may yet get out of the notion before that time arrives but that is my calculation at present. We have a Singing School at Mt. Pleasant We have our School made up by Subscribers. Our Teacher charges $15 for thirteen lessons. Our Teacher is old J. L. Boston. Brother he is a splendid singer. He throughs in Sundays free and sings twice a week. We have nice slaying Snow it is almost boot top deep in the fields where it has not blown off, but the wether is nice and warm over head. I want you to write when you go start for some new climate and let me know and if I can possibly go I will go with you. I am ready at any time according to my will to leave this cold country and go where I won't freeze my toes when I go after a load of wood.

By Ging goes it has been so cold here that it would shove a man to stick his head out of doors but I have stood the cold better than I anticipated. I have been trying to buy some calves and shotes, but the hogs all died with the Collery, and Lucky bought all the Bulls last Spring and made stag's of them so there is no calves in this neighborhood, and what there is, is of a Scrub Stock. And calves so small

13

that half of them I can by the tail and through over a six rail fence but you cant get them much short of Seven Dollars a head. Cattle and hogs are both very scarce in this settlement. Mothers hogs died but three. She killed her fattening hogs to keep them from dying, and I have no doubt if she would have tried to fatten them most likely she would lost all of them. Jane I always fulfill my promises if they are sometimes a long way off. them picture looked so much like a seven year old boy that I once was a going to burn them but Mother finaly persuacuded me out of the notion, as she does in everything else. I have now come to be a Bachelor the rest of my days If I cant get the one I want with out an Irish row I will not have any, but to tell the fact I had no notions of getting married as some suspicious persons thought. I am going to Ottumwa next Spring and hire a nigger to cook for me and fill the place of a woman and one thing I can do, I can turn this off whenever I get tired of them. I have queer ideas in my head concerning my local affairs. I must close as this is the last bit of paper I have and when I will get some more but I dont know no more but believe me to be your affectionate Brother Elias W. Shearer to S. I. and E. J. Shearer

March the 1st AD 1858

Dear Brother it is with pleasure that I sit down to write you a few lines to inform you that I and the rest of the friends are in tolerable good health with the exceptions of som of the neighbors. Rosy Mcvey has a tolerable sick child; Luis Lucky is not yet able to work I have wrote to you about the deaths and sickness of this neighborhood but I cannot tell whether you got the letter or not.

Henry Fleming's wife deceased first Geo. W. Mcvey deceased secondly Rosy McVey's daughter thirdly, by name (Peachy P. Mcvey) with others too tedious to mention. Sickness Donitia E. Mcvey was taken by with a Disease but I can not tell you what it is. This girl is a Daughter of Rosy Mcvey - so ends the Chapter

I am a going to go too Kansas. I expect to start next week if the rest gets ready. Mother says she would like to see you so no more at present
Simeon Shearer to Silas I. Shearer
Please write me a letter for I have not heard from you for nine months.

(Drawings on the bottom of this letter)

July the 18, 1858

Dear Friend it is with pleasure that we sit down to write you a few lines to inform you that we are well at present We hope that these few lines may find you enjoying the same blessing O yes O Yes we forget to tell you that we was at a Wedding last Sunday O Yes Silas you out to been there You cant gess where it was it was at the White House O gets it if you can but we are afraid that you cant Well if you can well all you it was Widow Ver Shearer and the widower Watkins was married we had a fine time there was between fourty and fifty took supper there and we had a fine time that night there was eleven there but Catharine was there but she was with her Deare but you cant gess how it was . . . .   you would like to now Well Dutch comes here yet but July she has get the suck fore a while for his cousin has got him but she is a going to dase before long Well Sarilda sayes she is a wating for you but we will tell you because she cant get any body else Uncle Andrew Shearer was here John and Nancy was here to and Eliza went home with them Well the singing we had a good dose of it the meeting house was full and we had Shilies Coundan to sing four us and we are a going to here a singing on the tenth of August and we would like if you and that other fellow can come for that and if cannot you must send us a letter

We must quit writing O yes we wood tell you that your folks is well and Uncle Andrew has bought a team Well I believe that all but remain your friends until death so read it if you can.

Amy Davis to Silas
Ady Paul to Silas
July Wellmas to Silas
Rebecca to Silas
Serilike E. Thurison to Silas
GoodBye SS

State of Iowa Wappelo Co
Sept the 25th 1858

Dear Brother It is with pleasure that I embrace the present opportunity to inform you that I am well at this time and hope these few lines will find you injoying good health Times is hard Money Scarce And can not Be got I am going up there this Fall or winter if nothing happens more than I know of now I would come up this fall but I cannot get any money for times are so hard When I go up it may be possible that I will stay all winter and go to school up there so know more youres with respect Simeon S. Shearer

Baah baah baah; you are the man that butted the bull off of the bridge and bellowed

Part of bottom letter missing

October the 25th AD 1858
State of Iowa Wappelo County

Sir I received your letter dated the 14th AD 1858 & mailed on the 15th AD 1858. I received the letter on the 25th 1858 and I was very glad to hear from you and the rest of the friends. You gave me the price of produce and I will give it in return. Wheat is worth $1.00 to $1.25 cts per bushel Corn $.25 to .30 cts per bushel Oats $0.50 cts per bushel potatoes three bushels of potatoes is worth one $1.00 Beef Cattle is worth $0.02 cts per lb on foot and all sold at that rate Hogs is worth $3.75 to $4.00 per hundred lbs. Mutton is worthe eating that's so. Dear Brother I take my pen in hand to inform you that I am well the rest of the friends are all well at present It would please me if these lines will find you and family enjoying good health You wanted to know something about that lot in shake rag I will tell you all I know about it. Uncle Andrew was in Ottumwa and asked about it but there was no . . . on this lot as they could not find any thing about it so it is all right You wanted to know where Alfred & Zebulon is I can tell you to a minute they are in Kansas by this time if they had no bad luck Zebulon came back this fall but left at Columbia City in the bends off the Missouri river below St Joseph Uncle Andy moved them out there and has not returned yet They started to Kansas on the 9th AD 1857. You look on the map of the States and just below St. Joseph in the bend of the river and there is Uncle Bob Hays lives, Zebulon says that there is peace in Kansas. I will tell you how peace come Capt Montgomery was sick and not expected to live when the pro slavery chaps come to the Capts

16

house they took all of his Stock and even his furniture and gave him so many hours to leave in and if he was found in the territory, they would take his scalp. He sent and got his nearest neighbor to haul him away then the Captain said if God spared him to live he would make them to think of it So he got well and made up a Company of twelve sharp rifflemen with some soldiers with Muskets and put out. The party had several little battles but Montgomery & Bane so completely whiped the other party so bad that they agreed to make peace so they set a day to meet and consult one withe another and when the partys met Old Bob Hays was therein They agreed to defend one an other and catch all the horse theives that they could I will give you the .... of the day all that I can say that the Democrats elected every Candadate that they had on the track and it rather gets the republicans down in the mouth.

If I under stand you right For July Ann cares no more for that Pretty woman than I care about Snakes By the long tow rope July Ann Has one of the bigest Boy, was since Adam was a Yearling. I say the God of the high has looked down upon you and Your Woman Amen & Amen Write soon write the Truth about matters and anything. The Shanghai Chickens are all to go in a few days. There are but few duck legged that they cant throw them on. I will bet a pint of Paddys eye water on it. Jordan and July Ann have a boy.

My dear beloved son I want you to come down if you can and see henry perry. Catherine to S I Shearer So no more but remember your affectionate brother.

From S. S. Shearer to S. I. Shearer

December the 26th AD 1858
State of Iowa Wappelo County

Dear brother I take this present opportunity to inform you that I am well at present the friends are all well as far as I know and I hope these few lines may find you and the rest of the friends in good health My long continuance but short distance from you makes me very inquisitive about you welfare

Times are hard here Money scarce and everything else is scarce Wheat is worth $1.15 cts per bushel Corn is worth from $0.65 to 75 cts per bushel and Pork is worth $3.50 to $4.50 cts per cwt We received a letter from little Robert Hayes Corn is worth $.50 to 0.60 cts per bushel Flour is worth $5.00 per cwt fresh pork is worth $5.00 per cwt (that is in the south part of Kansas) I am going to school this Winter A school Miss is teaching the school by the name of Mary Demon

There is a kind of fever here that I am afraid it sweep its Thousand It is called the Pikes Peak fever it is to be richer gold mines that California ever was. Peter Shearer is a going to the Peak next Spring, write as soon as you get this letter, write and let me know whether you are going out to the new California or not if you are you can get to go with Pete Shearer for he is trying to make up a Company to go out there next Spring. And whether you are Married or not for every Sunday a dozzen girls ask me whether you are married and I cant answer the question correctly. Thursday I will be Seventeen and I am a little the best man of my age that ever crossed my path I will inform you that Sir Pretty Girls are plenty down here I was at a party the other night I and Wilson Drake went down in a Sleigh at a party the other night I and Wilson Drake went down in a Sleigh and coming home our horse run away. He run from Old Hampson Smiths to Huffaker which is about one mile we was in the sleigh and at Old Hawthorn he tried it again but we turned him out of the road and run him against the fence when we got out I have been to three partys this Fall and I expect to go to another party New Years Eve at John Phelpses and I expect to play the cl ....1 and turn up jack If you want to write to Zebulon direct your letters to Smithton or Laport Post Office Donathan Co Kansas Territory I want you to write of the day tell E. T. Day to write again if he pleases tell C. T. McCord to write if he will Tell J. W. Day to write if you will Sir Write soon and dont Delay I wrote you a letter some time ago and have got no answer So no more at present but remains your affectionate Brother From S. S. Shearer to S. I. Shearer
Hurah for Pikes peak
Lots of doodles and drawing of a bird

State of Iowa Wappelo County
Fryday August the 5th AD 1859

Dear Brother it is with pleasure that I embrace the present opportunity to inform you that I and the rest of the friends are in tolerable good health and I hope these lines will find you and the rest of the friends injoying good health. I received your letter July the 3rd dated June the 18th and was sorry to hear that you had been sick but was glad to hear that you are restored too health and that you had a friend too take care of you. When you are away from home it is a true saying that we owe our respect to those who does us a favor and we ought to repay they in the best way we know how, and so indulge to do Silas, I have sat down here in order to write you an answer to the letter you wrote but I am almose ashamed to write to you after I was neglecting it so long There is considerable of sickness among Children John Shearer lost one of their Children Two more of them was sick, but

18

recovered. Peter Shearer's little boy was sick and not expected to live but he got well little Henry Perry has been sick but he is getting well.

I will give you the price of produce flour is on the fall at $3.25 to $3.75 per CWT Corn is worth $1.00 per bushel Oats is worth I do not know what for there is none sold but I can give you the price after awhile when the Oats is threshed Pork is worth 12 1/2 cts per lb. beef cattle is worth from 1 1/2 to 2 1/2 cts per lb on foot butter is worth 12 1/2 per lb eggs is worth 5 cts per doz. There is a two days meeting begins tomorrow at five OClock PM there will be a basket meeting beginning a week from tomorrow at 11 OClock AM it is to be in the grove where George Couger once lived Duncan Risley lives there now. William Wheeler & David Couger is here now they have just come from Kansas and say crops are very good out there They say the people are all well out there. Zebulon went to Salt Lake this Spring but when David Couger left Kansas he had got as far back as to big blue river He went through with a Government team Alfred is working at a Steam Mill in Columbus City at $1.50 Cts per day he did have a grocery out there but sold it If you want to write a letter to Alfred or Zebulon Direct your letter to Warthena post office Donathan County KA Elisabeth Hays is married she married a man by the name of Edward Roberts I just weigh 140 lbs and am five feet nine inches high and measure 34 inches around my breast close up to my arms and measure 26 1/2 inches just above my hips and am not broke too ride So No More Yours with respect Simeon S. Shearer to Silas I. Shearer Excuse my bad writing for it is a goos quile feather pen I expect to come up there this fall

November the 9th AD 1859

Dear Brother
It is with pleasure that I embrace the present opportunity to inform you that I am not very well at this time the cause of it is on the account of fire. About 12 OClock Wm Erskin living where Jacob Cowger once lived, started with some fire to fire a land he was breaking and accidentaly a coal of fire fell off of the chunk he was carrying and set (the wind being high) the weeds on fire which caught the grass and burned, (the wind being in the South) up toward our Stable and Hay. No one of us were at home at the time except Bartmas but Lewis Lucky soon come to his assistance but all was in vain The old Straw pile and rails caught fire and there being some high dry weeds between the stable and straw pile on flash and all was over. The two person above name did not try the virtue in water but applied boards very manly. The hay and stable and grainery caught fire and was consumed nothing being saved except horses and harness. The fire crossed the State road by our gate and come very nigh burning Uncle Valentines

house and came as nigh to Slaters Stables but the fire that I fought got out the same day and came nigh burning Peter Shearers fence which caused hard work and a heap of it. But that is not all on that same day fire got into John Hagen and his sons farms burned up the old mans house so did it the young mans house which was a fine frame house worth about $2,000 The ground is eceeding dry for there has not been any rain since Uncle Perry was here Uncle Andrew dont know what too do for he had about 1000 rails burned in that same Catastrope. The friends are all in good health I wrote to you that I was comeing up there this winter I am trying all the time but times are so hard I have got no money as yet to go on but write as soon as this comes to hand and write me a way bill so that I can come and cross the river on a bridge or dam for ferries will be froze up so no more.

Yours as ever Simeon S. Shearer

Write soon and dont delay Give my respect to all

Nice drawings on bottom of letter and Silas I. Shearer written in fancy lettering.

Saturday evening November the 27th 1859

Dear brother and sister It is with great pleasure that I this pleasant Saturday night have the opportunity of writing a few lines to inform you that I & the rest of the friends are enjoying good health at this time and hope those lines will find you both enjoying good health but I expect the work that you do could be done in a little while by a single man but I do not blame you for it at all for when you hear of my wedding you may just set your heel down that I will not work for six weeks What, too leave a new married wife and good looking Too Now Sister a few words to you I did not think you would serve me so for Elizabeth Jane if you would just have made it known if no other way but by letter it would do for I did want to marry tolerable bad but the match is broken to my Sorrow Oh Elizabeth Jane how can you serve me so for to rove the wide world over with a man that you dont know Sayes Elizabeth Jane to her lover (which is me) you may do the best you can and I will rove this world over for the sake of my Irish man but to return to the subject on which you wished for me to write and that is the price of produce Flour is worth $2 to $2.50 Corn is worth 15 cts to 20 cash Wheat is worth 50 & 60 Cts per bushel Potatoes is worth 25 &30 Cts per bu Oats is worth from 15 to 20 Cts on the account of it being so light Fat Hogs is worth from 3 1/2 to 4 Cts per lb on foot Eggs 10 Cts per dozen Butter is worth 15 cts per pound. Whether it will pay you to bring down a load of produce or not I cant tell but I believe after awhile I believe it will be a good price. I expect you have a good looking wife according to what Uncle Perry said but whether she has a good

20

looking man or not is for Elizabeth to Say Silas I know Jane is good looking not only good looking but beautiful for I know a pretty girl by the name of Sarah Jane McCord and she is good looking. I expect to pay you a visit this Fall but I do not know exactly whether I will be there this fall just now or not. It is Nine OClock I guess I will close excuse my Scribeing and bad Spelling for I have wrote in a hurry so no more youres as ever From Simeon S. Shearer For Silas I S. Elizabeth J Shearer

Good night Brother and Sister for it is bed time

Write as soon as this come's to hand Drew picture of leaf

Hurrah for Iowa Republican State Officers and Gov A. C. Dodge is candidate for U. S. Senator

Uncle Andrew has had the sore eyes for about three months but they are getting better but he can not see to read or write

I sent my respect to all especially Sister Elizabeth Jane Shearer

State of Iowa Wapello County
February the 22nd A.D. 1860

Honoured Brother & Sister - It is with a becoming reverence and Brotherly affection on this account of separation that I attempt to address a few lines to informing you that the friends and myself are enjoying good health and I hope these lines Though awkwardly wrote will find you enjoing the same great blessing of our Creator. Times are hard money scarce but prospects for the better. Produce corn is at 20 Cts Cash of Oats and Wheat I do not know the price. We have had the fairest winter here I have ever witnessed. Until now it is raining and the roads are muddy. If any more letters comes up there send them to competiness and oblige your brother excuse my writing and turn over. (Next Day) You may read this to my adopted sister or you may not just as you please. Whether Uncle Andrew will write to you I cannot tell for he is as curious and peevish as he was when you was at home. Him and Mother is the most pettish coupple I ever but this is nonsense. Silas I am going to school this winter to a young man by the name of Thos A. Creamer, a great and latin schollar. I am studying Spelling reading Ciphering and Kirkhams Grammar. I have omited Geography for this Winter. I am on the 303rd page in arithmetic page 261 3rd sum Amisred 25 lbs at 18 Cts and 40 at 25 Cts per lb what is answer Proud of this mixture operation 25 lbs at 12 Cts per lb 25x12=$3.00 25x18Cts per lb 25x18=$4.50 40 lb at 25 Cts per lb 40x25=$10.00 Divide this whole cost by the whole number of simples the quotient will be the mean price. If you have a sum that you think will puzzle me send them by letter to me and I will try and send you an answer. Uncle Andrew is going to the Missouri next Fall to live. Write soon. Sister I want you to write and don't keep putting me off from one time to another. Yours as ever Simeon S. Shearer to S.I. & E. J. Shearer Don't forget to write.

State of Iowa Wappelo County
March the 12th AD 1860

Honored Brother and Sister It is with great delight that I embrace the present opportunity of addressing a few lines to you to inform you that I and the friends are all well at this time, hopeing these uninvited lines will find you both enjoying a portion of health Times are very hard money scarce but prospects for the better. I dont know the exact price of Produce Corn is a good demand at twenty one cts per bushel Wheat about 75 to 80 Cts per bushel Oats 25 to 30 cts per bushel. Some of the people are sowing their Wheat but we have not sowed any yet. I am writing this in order to let you know that if you want a school taught up in your neighborhood I will teach it for you if you will let me know of it I will not try to get a certificate of the Superintendant of the County for I do not believe I could get a Certificate for teaching Grammar & Geography but I believe by studying with the Class I can teach it and as to Geography most any person (so I am told) can teach it that can pronounce the hard word. As to writing this is a specimen of a running hand. I can write a better copy hand than this or a running hand. As to Rays Arithmetic part third I am master of it all except the last page. I would swear that I could work them. I can teach Spelling and Reading. I will teach what I have named for reasonable wages, but the School will have to be a Sub-scription School as I said I would try to get a certificate. I will do the very best I can for the benefit of the Children provided I get a school. I will go up there as soon as you answer this.

Write soon and don't delay

These favors I ask for a Brothers sake

yours as ever Simeon S Shearer to Silas I & Elizabeth J Shearer

Excuse my scribing for this time.

Pompey was stabbed by Septimins standing on the Shore of Egypt

Sunday October the 14th 1860

Again I am constrained to take my seat with the determination of writin you an answer to your letter that you about two months in writing For your first was dated April the 2nd 1860 continuing up June the 17th 1860 much longer than Douglas' Two days speech in the Senate in May 1860. But such a letter does not astonish me at all for such Greek and Latin Scholar's as are in Story county, it is supprising it comes like a whirlwind upon my mind But with a powerful exhertion I withstood the Storm of your letter. Ever since we have had correspondence things have went off smoothly until 1860. When your powerful scholarship broke forth from your talented mind through such a mouth of wisdom as yours, I could fancy I saw a tremendous cloud of smoke and a numbling as the sound of many water's. All from a mortal man, if the earth was inhabited by such vas monsters the earth would real on its axis. Your sum of your nine figures I did not try to set in order as any school boy can set them down with ease. your other example of that sinking ship with a hole twelve feet square and one board 16 ft long and 9 ft wide now this is a question of inconsistency for how could a crew cut a board one time where there is a twelve foot hole, for it would sink in 15 seconds, so with inconsistency answer your inconsistent questions. I have no more to add.

The political issue of the day is discussed every week. There was a republican mass meeting in Marysville yesterday and there was an iminense company which was addressed by Mr. Lottsperich and Dickson of Ottumwa

So Lincoln is the President he will give us all a Farm I add no more
Simeon S. Shearer
Elizabeth I cannot write to you now, write soon sister S.S.S.
Three of Uncle Pettys family is sick with the fever
Take no offence at what I have said

January the 13th AD 1861

Dear Brother and Sister

It is with pleasure that I imbrace the present opportunity of informing you that we are all well at the present time. The intent of my writing is to inform you that we have sold our possessions here to Mr. John W Rouse and David M. Rouse Uncle Andrew did not sell none but his and Mothers and my part in the estate with Elizs Barteman Andrew and Elias part, your share is left for you to sell and if you want to sell you may set your own price. Your interest is one eighth of the 140 acres. If you want to sell write your price and send it by letter Our intention is to go to Kansas next Fall although we have to give possession here in the Spring. Uncle Andrew has rented a farm of Hesakiah Creamer Eight miles South of this on the Railroad. I was struck with supprise on reading of the Birth of a Nephew as you stated Tell him about his Uncle. Mother is well at present. I will close with the expectation of an answer.

Grandfather Shearer is Dead.

I am with respect your unworthy Brother

Simeon S. Shearer to Silas I and Elizabeth Shearer

Camp Lyon Birds Point, Missouri
Saturday, October the 26th, 1861

Dear Bro & Sister

I address this to you to let you know that I am well and in the Army and expect to stay in the Army for some time likely for I have been advised by my best friends to go in the military school at West Point as soon as the War is over. These friends knowing my disposition think it profitable for me and likely for the Government. I have time to meditate on these things. Before I do this is the gloomyist hour of the War. Soon there must be a dredful and effedual struggle for union for if the war is not vere nearly wound up by next Spring then the War will be prolonged for many years for there is a possibility of the Independence of the so called Southern Confederacy being acknowledged by the European powers. But I am willing to serve out my time for the benefit of my Country. We have seen hard service in our travels. Four months we was not still but going all the time. Our longest march was from Pilot-Knob Mo to Cape Girardeau on the Miss River. This was an Eight day march. We have been here one month. Our Regt is greatly reduced. It once contained 1000 men now we can muster for service 400 men I suppose we will go to St. Louis to recruit. Our Regt is one of the oldest in service I must close these remarks for the present. I want you to write soon as this comes to hand so no more But remains yours as ever Simeon S. Shearer to S I. & E J Shearer

P.S. direct letters to S. S. Shearer, 2nd Regt Iowa Vol Co K via St. Louis   I am well.

I send my respect and love to all the friends Birds Point is strongly fortified Good Bye

To John Shenkle Father-in-law of Silas Shearer
"Cure for the fistula or pollevil"

Take one oz of Cantharides
One Half a pint of turpentine
1 oz Camphor
1 oz or corrosive sublimate pulverized
mix and let it stand a day
Use about 2 tabe spoonful on each side and bathe well with a hot iron
do this once a day till your medicine is all used
Bled moderately on the 1st 5th and 10th day
give three or four does of Sulphur
If broke ride this medicine with a Syringe if running
The same medicine for the fistula if running
Wash the sore well with soapsuds inside and outside eastell soap is the best
Keep your horse in the dry while using this medicine feed but little corn
Wash first before you use the medicine
When done using the medicine greeze with lard to prevent scaring
When you done your medicine put it in a bottle and shake it a little before you use it.

As for Simeon he is not here he volunteered and went with the first Company from Ottumwa he was at St. Joseph Mo the tenth of July but now at St Louis he is in the second regiment of Iowa I have had four or five letters since he left One letter said he was sick now but now he sais he is well Yesterday the fourth company from Wapalo past here it was a horse company   Simeon hates the name of sessionists I have give up of going to Kansas this Fall   Times hard and money scarce and I would have to pass threw Missouri and I am not friend to no trator and I would likely get into a scrape I was agoing to write more but my eyes pains me so that I will quit
We are all well yours as ever
A and E Shearer to S Shearer
Write as soon as this letter comes to hand

Date & Place Unknown

Well Father the tickets you sent me did not reach here untill yesterday which was Sunday after the Election. I was very well pleased with them the day of Election I could not get but one kind of a Story County ticket so I did not vote a Story County ticket I took a Polk County ticket and put Story on it and scratch the County Officers off and went for Tuttle if Tuttle had have came out as an indepenant Candidate Stone would have been no where with him among the Soldiers Tuttle had a big name among the Soldiers Story County boys are fiew and Scatering in this Regt I am the only one in Co K at the present time our Co has nine privates two Corporals Ordly Sargant and two Commisioned Officers with the Regt at the present The 18th Army Corps goes a head of us with the Exceptions of one day and then we turned to the right to go threw a little town to drive the Rebles out off it Gene Washburn and Staff was the advance when we came to town the pickets fired on them and they Skedaddled back where they could be protected The 11th Wis Regt was throwen out as Skirmishers and we was brought up in line of battle to Support them We got three or four of the Whelps that was all we could find the rest maid for better quarters Negroes say they was about 25 of them the 18th Army Corps is Skirmishing with them. At every town they come to the Rebls down here are principle all mounted they attacted our train the other day and they took 12 wagons but the guard soon made them give them up I want you to let me know how the Election went and the Majority if you know it I must close for this time
youres as ever S. I. Shearer to B. Shenkle

McDowell Coillege Saint Louis, Mo
Monday, January the 27th 1862

Dear Brother and Sister
Yours of the 20th Inst is before me. I am well and enjoying all the happiness that the Articles of War allows a Soldier. You have been very neglectful from some cause or other unknown to me for it has been about two or three months since I write to you. But I suppose you are excusable. As far as money is concerned I cannot assist you for a Month at least for on our last pay day I sent my allowance Home by Express from which I heard today by a letter from home. I even the help I will do for you what I can next pay day if we are where we can express money so write as soon as you get this and let me know the nearest express office to you. I am send you my miniature in a few days but it will be small so that I can send it by mail. (Have the miniature) And if I send it keep it from the gaze of the fairsee for I confess my Homiliness.

Who is there in Story County to enquire after the couple time Boy except-it-is-yourself and Janie and Uncles Wesley and Perrys families. I may pay you a visit after the Rebellion is crushed if I do not go to Califorania or some other Seaport. Here in the Army is the] place to spend money. I loaned a part of my first months pay and have notnor ever will receive a farthing from them for one is discharged and other in the Hospital. Our institution - the College is rapidly improving it is still thronged with students. But before I proceed I will State to you our situation. We are guarding Rebel Prisioners in the old McDowell College on 8th S Gratiot Street. When we first received those Prisioners they numbered 1300 Now 1100 the decrease is owning to the taking of the oath of allegiances by some three or four Hundred of them. But still Missouri sends in her disloyal inhabitants for to have them educated according to a theory used by Professor J. W. Tuttle [our Col] He has Boys assistance to help him in his duty. We teach them that Uncle Samuel is not to be fooled with and that they have to submit or somebody will get hurt. From reports we will soon leave for down river and is also stated that we are to be the advance guard of the Grand Army that will move against Columbus, Ky the Rebel stronghold of the West. We are reputed as being one of the best drilled Regt's in the Service. How true it is I am Dammedable to say. I must quit as I have nothing more to write but write soon for if it was not for my Correspondence which is numerous I would see no pleasure at all. My little Blue Eyed Girl favors me with a letter frequently I desist Remaining as Ever Simeon S. Shearer To Silas and E. J. Shearer

P.S. Directo to Co "K" 2nd Iowa Inft Via Saint Louis, Mo

My love and respects to all Enquiring Friends.

All we ask is to be led against our Enemy and test the matter. Onward to Victory or Death is my Motto

Addressed to Edenville, Marshall County, Iowa (Edenville is now known as Rhodes)

Simeon Shearer was wounded in battle and Died March 25, 1862 and burial at Cairo, Illinois in Military Cemetery.

Saturday - April 12, 1862

I received a letter from a man Simeon <u>nows</u> he was not expected to live and he said he wanted me to come down immediately. I got on the Cars on the third of April on the Fifth I landed at Caro and walked six mile up the river to Mounds City where Simeon had been buried about a week before I got there. They had kept him about five days for me. He became in a putrified State so they buried him. The tolerable Agent had a Cofen made and buried about four feet under ground so I left him buried at Mounds City.* In the Hospital the graveyard a tollerable pretty graveyard. There he rests until Gabriel shall sound and bid the

dead awake Blessed are they that have a part in the first reserection Where I verily believe that he is now in the realms of bright glory where he won't have to do what he had to do. Where there will be all Joy and Peace. I was talking with his nurses They said he said he well satisfied with his fate. He said he would like to be at home. I know I can't so I am satisfied. They said he was as quiet as a lam with a smile on his countenance. They said his last words was I am satisfied with my fate is my Country free and bid them all farewell and fell asleep in Jeses We morn not as those that have no hope and all we have to say the Lord giveth and the Lord taketh but blessed is the name of the Lord. He can't come to us but we can go where he is. We are all well and hope that you are all enjoying good health. Now we commend you to God and hope you will try to meet your Brother in heaven Herein where there will be no more sorrow nor harking of presence. He was born December the 30th 1841 Died March 25, 1862 I started on the third I got home on the tenth. I heard the bombardment of island no ten. We gained the victory. Read this and let the friends reread it and C. Shearer S Shearer Write soon and often.
*U. S. Military Cemetery - Cairo, Illinois

June 22, 1862

It is with pleasure that I take my pen in hand to inform you that we are all well at this time and hoping these times will find you all in joining good health. I received your letter I write this in answer to that letter. You wanted to know where Simeon fell He fell just before he Clim the Wall of Fort Donnalson. His thigh was broke five inches below the rite hip. The second Iowa regulars chosen to storm the works supported by the 52 Ind Regiment 25 Ind Reg, Iowa Regt 121 Iowa Lowman had command of the brigade. They went in the works by Battalion because there was no room for Regiment to go in so they had to go by Battalion. Two Battalions makes one regiment. Colonel Tuttle was asked whether he could storm the Fort in fifteen minutes. He replied was his men [don't forget my regiment] to support him. Grant said he could have fifteen reg if he wanted them so he supported him four other reg. Tuttle he went to his Reg told his Reg where he wanted them to go Attention and they was all ready to March Tuttle in the lead they marched steady up the hill without firing at us Clim the Wall and drove the scape galesses for Geaesh is Treason.

Treason is Hanging therefore they are scupe galisis from there outward in trenchment in to there inner intrenchment. There the Q Reg stood between two batteries until they went back and called for the Seventh Iowa Reg drove from behind the 2 Reg from and from there battery (this battery was to the rear and to a little to the left of 2 reg when in the work and one in front. the reason they caled the R Reg the 52 Ind Reg refused to go in They cald the R Reg galient They

28

marched threw the 52 Ind Reg and went into the intrenchment and drove them from the Battery behind the 2 Regiment in to the inner entrenchment and then 2 did not suffer so much. The 2 left Lewis mad. They fough as if they was mad they went to take it and they did take it. James Shearer is in the 52 Infl Reg they went all threw the Pitsburg fight. None Hurt. William Jenkins and William Jacob Mower allso went through walk trown an was held at Pitsburg. Alfred Chill and B. Hays They down in Tennessee in the first Tenn Calvrey. Chill and Lowyer is at Ft. Scot Kans. Barty and Elias is in the Seventeenth Reg and the last I herd from him was South of Barinth thirty or fourty miles. Today I herd they was at Barinth again and was ordered to St. Louis. Elias was left at St. Louis Hospital sick but not bad. I have not herd from him for four weeks. I send a letter but directed it to his Reg I sent a letter Post Hospittle where he was left but I have not got a letter from him yet. There in _____ decision if you want to write direct your letter to Benton Barracks, Mo Seventeenth Reg Co E in care of Capt. Ping. That is the headquarters of the Western Army and it will be forwarded to the Regiment. Grain looks tolerable good Spring Wheat not so good Corn looks well I want you to be posted in the apple business and write to me every two weeks and give me the price offer the middle of July and as much sooner as you can offner as you want to and oblge me for am agoing in St. Louis again. Now don't forget what I told you. Don't be alarmed be cause I come at the bottom of my paper.

Camp Burnside - Des Moines
September the 3rd 1862

Dear Companion

It is with pleasure that I take my pen in hand to inform you that I am well at present time and I hope that these few lines may find you in good health. I hope that Denver is well. I heard yesterday that you were all well. I would be glad to see you all but I expect it will be douhtful. I will get to for some time but live in hopes and take good care of yourself. The news is now that we will leave this week. When we will go is more than I know. The Colonel said this moring we were the best Company in the 23rd Regt. We get our Uniforms today and tomorrow we are mustered in the United States Service the boys are Principle we some have the Diahrea It seems as though am lost without my Jane and Denna Dau, Never so happy when I am with them. Well Jane I'll write you a few more lines this being the 21st. I have a chance of sending this early than I anticipated and by Cap Woodberry. He is going to leave us for good I presume. He says he wishes he could take us all with him. I will send ten dollars by him in this letter. It will be more safe with you than it will with me. I wish I had what was owen to me to send to you for I hainet any alarmed but what will be safe with you. You must excuse me if my letters are few for we are where there is Know mail line and we have to until a train goes back to send our letters. Yours as ever, S. I. Shearer

Keokuk, Iowa
September the 26th, 1862

My Dear Companion and Son It is with great pleasure that I embrace this present opportunity of informing you that I am well at the present time. Our boys are all well Uncle Pery he has that pain in his head but is not very bad yet. I hope that these few lines may find you in good health. We left Camp Burnside Sunday morning the 21st and landed here Thursday noon. We eat dinner Sunday noon at Rising Sun and then marched along to Mud Creek close to Heath Tavern where we staid all night. The next day we came to Prairie City where we got our Dinner. it was a free dinner and a very good dinner and after dinner our Leutenant Colonel gave us good advice. He said when we was down South we should live as though our Parents was watching over us and when we return home we must come like men. A Monday night we staid close to Monroe City and the next day we eat dinner in Pella and we staid all night close to the Nine Mile House and a on Wednesday we eat dinner in Oskaloosa and we reached Eddyville that Evening and the next morning at Six O'Clock we got on the Cares and reached Keokuk at noon. We leave here in the morning for St. Louis and the reports is that we go in Curtis'es Division. Some say we go to Rolla, Mo but that is uncertain. I think I seen William Bullock yesterday. He was so he could go about with a Croch and Cane. Bob Bailes is in our Tent now he was sent here to the hospital. There is several hundred sick and wounded Soldiers here in the Hospittal. I want to go to the Barracks today to see Uncle Andrew if he is there. I seen more pleasure that day I was at home with Genna and Denna than I have since I left. Tell Denna that his Papy would like to se him. I want you to be reconsiled and live in hopes for you Husband keeps you in his mind. If he can't be with you his love and affection is with you. I want you to live as though I was with you I want you to write to me when ever you can. A letter will give me great satisfaction. My Dear Jenna write soon. Direct your lettersto the Twenty Third Iowa Regiment, Company K.

St. Louis, Missouri. I must bring my letter to a close. Write soon my Dear. I remain your loving Husband untill Death.
From Silas I. Shearer to Elizabeth J. Shearer

Camp Schofield, St. Louis MO
October the 5th, 1862

Dear Companion It is again with pleasure that I embrace the present opportunity of informing you of my health which is not very good at the present time. I have been sick for pretty nigh every since I have been at St. Louis but I am getting better and probably will get along if nothing hapens. There is considerable Sicnes in our Regt at present. It is mostly measels there isent but few sick in our Company. There has been one death in Company A since we landed here. I hope these few lines will find you all in good health and the comforts of life surrounding you. Wels is fat and harty and enjoys himself very well and that is a blessing for him. Uncle Pery is not able for duty yet but I think he will be before long. When any one gets sick in Camp I can feel for them now. they have got to take things as they come. it is not like home but I got along but never want to be sick in Camp again so I will leave the balance for you to guess at if you are good at guessing. We are Provost Guards for the City and to guard prisenors. Our company garded prisenors yesterday The numbered betwixt Seven and Eight Hundred and this morning there was about 80 more brought in. We cannot tell how long we will remain here. We may remain here all winterand again we may not stay a week. The Officers in this City offers to bet all they are worth that peace will be declared in less than sixty days. Our Colonel sayes he will bet Six Hundred Dollars that we will discharged in less than Sixty days. There was about Seven Hundred Soldiers Sick and Wounded landed here day before yesterday and they all say it will end before that time if it would be so it would be a Gods blessing. There was one of my old schoolmates came to se my today He is a recruit for the first Iowa Cavalry. There is some more boys at Benton Barax that I know. Tom Colliar came to this City the other day Sick but not bad. I seen Uncle Andrew, Pete Shearer, and Henry Hufman, a Cousin by Marage and several others that I knew. I must bring my letter to a close. I want you to write and not wait for me to write and I will do the same. You do not know how much good a letter would do me and therefore I want you all to write. Write soon my dear. You and Denna are as dear to me at this time as ever you were. I still remain your loving husband untill death. Tell Denna his Pap would like to see him. Silas IShearer to E. J. Shearer

On same letter
Dear Father and Mother You must not think hard of me for not writing to you forget to here from me when even I write to Jane and times is such that I can not write often.
I still remain you Son
Silas I. Shearer Write Soon

Picture Union Flag with Statue
November 11, 1862

Dear Father and Mother For the first time I write you a few lines and I hope that these lines will find you in good health. You write a letter to Nelson and it was put in an envelope with the one that Jane sent to me. I Have not seen Nelson for four weeks. The Regiment moved a day or two after I took sick and I have not seen him since. I put the letter in a new envelope and put it in the office this morning and I suppose he will get it. The Reg is forty or fifty miles from here at present but they have orders to leave this week for Cape Gireardo. They is rumors of fifteen thousand Rebbels in that vicinity but it may all be flying reports. I would like to se Nelson but I do not know when I will get to se him. Uncle Pery and Downs once since I have been sick. I am here among Straingers and Ihave a very lonsome time of it but I am treated as well as could be expected in such a place. I want you to write to me and give me the <u>Prices</u>. I heard that they was agoing to draft in Iowa. Yours respectfully S I. Shearer to B. E. Shenkle

Arcade Hospital, Missouri
December the 9th, 1862

Dear Companion It is again I write you a few lines to answer to your letter which I received the Eighth. First one was dated the twenty third of last month and the other the 30th of the same and they gave me great satisfaction to hear that you are all well. I am still slowly on the mend and I think probably I will get well after while and I hope these few lines may find you in good health. I received a letter from Uncle Pery and Nelson the 8th Nelson wrote that he was getting better likely he will get home by the time you get this letter. He wrote that he was looking for his Discharge every mail. I am glad to heare such news because you need him at Home I am not so particular about going home since I heard that he had hopes of going Home. I do not expect that I will get to go home this time and if I only get Stout I am perfectly satisfied to stay. They applied for a discharge for me but the Doctors at the Reg did not do nothing with it. The Colonel was here

the other day and he said all the men that was not able to March he was going to send Home and send recruiting officers to recruit for the Regiment. We had Preaching here last Sunday for the first time. It is the first preaching I heard since I left Burnside and it maid me think of times past and you A times which I used to have in Iowa. I wish then that I was at Home so I could go to meeting. I have go so that I would like to go to meeting once and awhile. I am glad to hear that our Children are fat and harty. I would love to see Denna and the Babe. You wrote that you had not named the Babe yet. You wrote that you Mother wanted you to call it Elizaann. I donot like the name as well as I would Elen or Jane but name it what you please I want you to kiss Dennan and the Babe for me and tell Denna that his Pap is getting well and he would like to se him but do not know when he will get to see them for he is a good ways off but I think as often of you here as though I was with you at home. I wish that the War would end soon so we could return to our lovely families so that we could enjoy some pleasure. I did not write to you last week for I was looking for a letter. Henry Colson is here now I guess. The prospects bids fair for him to get a discharge He is not able to do any thing and I and him took a walk to a Store yesterday evening which was about a Quarter of a mile and that is the farthest I have been since the Hospital Since I have been sick The weather is fine here as I ever seen but it is not a healthy Country. I have nothing of importance to write You need not write any more letters until I write to you again. I suppose this Hospital will be broken up next week and where I will go I cannot tell. I want you to rest easy for I can get along some how another. You must excuse my bad writing this time. Oh yes I liked to forgot Aunt Sarah need not feel so big if Uncle Pery is in Office for he has to hold the Privates heads while they Shit. Perhaps you think I am Gassing but I have out long enough to know that, so no more present but remain your affectionate Husband untill Death.
Silas I Shearer to E. J. Shearer

Arcada Hospital, MO

Dear Brother it is with a degree of pleasure that I write you a few lines. I have described my health in Janes letters and so it is useless to put in this one but I hope that these few lines may find you in good health and spirit. I suppose you are quite lonesome since Nelson has left but I hope he will return soon in good health. It will soon be six weeks since I seen Nelson and I have not heard from him for three or four weeks and I would like to see him. I enjoyed myself very well while I was with the Boys but now it goes very slow and lonesome. I must tell you a little about the country. We are about sixty miles from the Mississippi River and it is nothing but hills and hollars. There is timber over the hills and the ground is covered with stone. Pilot Knob is about a mile and a half high that is to

the top of it and the iron cars runs to the top of it for the purpose of geting iron for it is an iron mountain. This is an iron country here. I have not seen any farming land since I have been in Mo. I must bring my letter to a close for I am getting tired. You must write so no more a present but remains yours as ever.
Silas Shearer to J. W. Shenkle
J. W. Shenkle was Silas Shearer's Brother-In-Law. Jane's Brother

Carter County Missouri
December the 25th 1862

Dear Companion it is again with pleasure that I write a few lines to let you know that I am well and hearty at this time and I hope that these few lines may find you all well. I must tell you something about our travels. We started from Arcada about two weeks ago and it rained very near all of the time and the watter raised and the roads got very bad that it takeing us four or five days to make the trip but finely got threw and we Staid at Patterson a few days and then we was ordered to March where we now lay. We left Patterson on Saturday morning and landed here on Wednesday Evening following. We are now in a secret hole but it is. We have a good battery with us and the Twenty Third it has to support the Battery providing it gets into a battle. It is the first Mo Battery one that Sigle had at the battle of Pea Ridge. They are all Brafs Cannon. Philander Smith took dinner with us today he is the same oald crank it is a great treat to se oald friends when a person is away from home. I must finish my letter to day is Monday the 29th inst. It is a hard place to write letters in the Army but I will write when ever I can. You must not think hard of me for not writing before this time for I will write whenever I can. I was on Picket and did not get off in time towrite yesterday It was the first time I ever was on guard of any kind. To day I am alone in my tent for the principal part of the company has gon out foraging. We hav to send two or three companys with the wagons in order to keep them from being captured by the guarilles which are very bad on the other side off the river. A train crossed the River for the above named purpose and the Rebels came on them and wounded four and taken the remainder of the Squad and teams. Our men killed two of there men Those men that was taking was off a Misouri Regiment but in our Brigade we do not know how soon we may be attacted but we will give them the best turn we have in the slop which I think will be pretty Good. There is between five and Eight Thousand troops here and twenty four pieces of Artilery and pretty good men to back them. The Twenty Third is all the young regiment here but the aritlerman thinks an awful site of it so it has a good name. That is all we want but how long they will keep it good is more than I can tell. They may run the first time the get in Battle I suppose you all know something about the Abolition papers. I know I remember that they used to read (whether they do now or not is

more than I can tell) the Democrats that goes to the Army soon changes to Abolitionist but it is to the contrary in our Regment. When we were at Ft. Des Moines two thirds of the Regment was Abolitionist and now it is hard to find them. They know now what Negroes are. I got a letter from Mother two or three weeks ago and they were all well. She said the Boys were well. Barty was sent to Keokuk untill he got well of his wound. She said Uncle Andrew was at St. Louis. Tell Turner I received a letter from him and I will answer it as soon as I can. I would like to see you all but it may be a good while before I will get home. About four weeks ago I took a change and I am getting as fat as a hog for we live like hogs. I got a letter from Bob Heath since I have been in the Army and they want my likeness. I suppose I will have to send it to them as soon as I can. When you write direct to S. Louis Co K 23 Reg, Iowa Volunteers. Tell Denna that his Pap has got well and he would like to se him. Write whenever you can and I will do the same. Send a stamp with the letter if you please and you will oblige me. I will have to quit my foolishness for you will get tired of reading it. So no more at present but remain your affectionate husband.
Silas I. Shearer to E. J. Shearer

Iron Mountain St. Francis Co Mo February the 2nd 1863

Dear Companion   It is once more that I embrace the present opportunity of adressing a few lines to you to let you know that I am well at present and I hope these few lines may find you all enjoying good health. I have sent my dress coat and a pair of gloves and a gold pen and holder the last named things you will find in the coat pocket and my cap I have sent also. These things will be sent to oald man Randles. The reason I sent my things to him is because Dave and Henry Perin sent theres to him and I thought it would not cost as much to send with them than to send by myself. I also sent thirty five dollars and I sent it in a package with some of the boys and it was directed to Leander Smith and you can get it from him. I will send to you what you have been wanting to see. I went to the office this morning and had my likeness taken and I will send it by mail in this letter and when you get it you must not imagine I have come home and take it to bed with you for you would be very apt to over lay it. I will send it without a case and if you want it in a case you will have to get one for it. The picture cost me one dollar but I thought you would not begrudge one dollar for such a picture. It is said to be a very good picture and the very image of me now I will expect to see your likeness in exchange for this. I received your very kind letter the 1 inst and it gave me great satisfaction to hear that you were all well. I would like to se Denna very much in fact I would like to se you all. There was quite an accident happened on this Railroad Road a day or two ago. A regment of infantry started for St. Louis on there way a tree fell acrost the track. It fell when the cars was about thirty yards off the spot so they could not stop and it threw boath locamotives off the track and it masht one all to pieces. How many cars was thrown off the track I can not tell but it killed several soldiers and wounded a great many more. I seen one of the men this morning in the depot that was killed. That Reg was the 24th Mo. I have not very much to write at this time for I wrote you and Father a letter two or three days ago but I must correct you in one thing and that is to you intrust in forming your letters. If you will set them a little more strait and not slant them so much you will write a great deal better this is for you intrust not for anyone not for anyone particular. Coffee is worth fifty cts per lb and tobacco is very high. Those five Cts plugs are worth fifteen cts per plug and other things are in proportion. I must bring my letter to a close. I will expect your likeness in a letter pretty soon. I would be very glad to se it but I would rather see you than to se your likeness but at it is I would be glad to se your likeness. From your loving Husband Silas I. Shearer to Elizabeth J. Shearer. You must excuse my bad writing and if it does not please you will I will quit writing.

Camp near West Plane Mo
February 7, 1863

Dear Companion It is again I write you a few to let you know that I am in tolerable good health and the boys are principly well. I hope these lines will find you all enjoying good health. I received from you dated January 4th it came to me the first inst and yesterday I received three more dated January the 12th, 15th, and 18th and I was glad to hear that you was all well. Such letters as that pleases me as long a I can heare of you enjoying good health. I can be satisfied. Nelson is at Prouton Hospital and that was the last I heard from him. I do not know how he is geting a long if you hear from him I want you to write to me and let me know how he is for I am a good ways from him. I wisht he was heare he could get to go home I think without a doubt but where it is it will probably be some trouble for him to get a discharge unless the Hospital is broke up. You said you had hired Jake to make that fence have him to put up so as it will turn stalk but I think there is nodought but he will and I want you to have the other fence repaired so as it will turn stalk Aunt Sarah wants the ground and I toled Uncle Pery that she could have it if he sayes anything to you about the ground tell her He can have it for he will stay there next summer. We have not been paid yet but prospects is fair. We signed the pay roll today and I presume we will be paid in a day or two. I am glad to hear that you got that land about paid for. You must not scant your self in

36

money matters although when ever you can convenyently pay the balance and lift the Mortgage and then you will know who the land belongs to. I will send you money when ever I can but where we are now it would be a difficult matter to send money for we cannot express money where we are now. I cannot tell how many letters I have received from you and I cannot tell how many I have written. It has been well nigh a month since I have written to you. I have two reasons for it one is we have been marching considerable and the other is my eyes are very weak and we are in so much smoke that I can not Se to write half of my time so you must excuse me for I will write when ever I can. I received that money you sent me and answered it. That was the last letter I have written to you. I received a letter from Elias and he said that him and Barty was well he said Barty was as fat as he ever seen him since he got well of his wound. We have had a pretty severe spell of wether here it snowed three or four days ago and then turned coald and has been coaled ever since untill today it has moderated and looks very much like falling wether. I have seen Squire Newhouse and Charly Barker since we came here. They are in the 22nd Iowa Reg. Ever once and a while we run against someone we know. I am in a inefs (tent) with Uncle Pery Dave and Henry Perin and Melven Barbee. We have a jolly old set of fellows. I would like to Se you all I would like to Se Lewis Denna very much. Tell him when his Pap gets home he will sing for him an Sis I want you to writ to me whenever you can and I will do the same So no more at present but remains your affectionate Husband Silas P. Shearer to E. J. Shearer

Pens slaches

Iron County M.O.
February the 24th 1863

Dear Companion It is again I write you a few lines to let you know that I am well at present and I hope that these few lines may find you all well and enjoying great pleasure. I received two letters yesterday from you one was dated January the 25th and the other one February the 8th and I was very glad to hear from you and to hear that you was well. You wrote you did not get very many letters from me I suppose you have not for we have been marching for eight or ten weeks and I have not wrote many letters. When ever we would stop I would be tired and I would want to rest but you need not think by my negligence in writing that I think any less of you for I would give considerable to be with you. I suppose you thought you would have me to write whether I wanted to or not by sending me a paper and an invelop it seems as though you are bound to hear from me someway or another but I have plenty of paper and invelops and money. We was paid up to the first of January and I got forty six dollars and eighty cts and If you be a right

good womin I will send you some of it as soon as I can. We are within four or five miles of Pilot Knob but we are not alowed to go to town. If I can get a chance I will send my money home before we leave here. Reports say that we are to go down the River probably to Vixburgh. You wrote you had heard that ten of our company had went out on a Scout and had taken four thousand dollars from a womin that was the first I have heard of it. In the first place there is no such a man as Wickersham in our company nor never has been and the next place there has not been any of our boys out on a scout so you can set that down as a fals report. You need not believe half the news you heare. I was very glad to get to See a lock of Dennas and the babes hare. It pleased me very much to se the children hair but I would be a great deal better pleased to get to se them and you. You said you would send me your likeness if I wanted it I would be very glad to see it. I will expect to se you in you miniture likeness before many many weeks roles around and I would like to see the childrens also. I will send myne to you as soon as I can get it taken but I cannot tell how soon that will be. I intended to send you one or two blankets and my dress coat and afew other things home when I got threw to the railroad but we have a case of the Smallpox in our company. I has been in the reg for a bout two month and so I will not send my blankets for fear I will send the Smallpox home. I would not send them home for considerable when I was in the Hospital I was exposed to the small pox and I was vaxinated imediatly after the found out what was the matter and it worked out well on me. You had all better be vaxinated as soon as possible for the Smallpox will be mighty apt to go threw Iowa for someone or other will be mighty apt to send it home. If I was somewhere so as I could take care of myself I would not mind haveing them half so bad. I heard from Nels today and the man said that he had started to go to the Reg by the way of Rolla His discharge was made out and sent to him and I thinkthat he will get it before he gets to the Reg. If not he will get it soon after he gets to the Reg for he will get it soon after he gets to the Reg for heis not fit to be one of Uncle Sams boys. I would be very glad to heare of his getting to go home. This is the paper that you sent to me and I will send the Invelop with the paper. I must bring my letter to a close for I am for I am tired. I was patching my close this forenoon. I will write soo I want you to write whenever you can. I would like to se you all very well but it may be a good while yet So no more at present but remains you affectionated husband.
Silas J. Shearer to Eliza beth J. Shearer

Iron Mountain Iron County Mo
February 27, 1863

Dear Companion It is again I write you a few lines to let you know that I am well at present and the health of the boys are very good and I hope these few lines will find you all enjoying good health. We was paid a week or two ago and I received forty six dollars and 80 cts and today I expressed thirty five dollars home. Five or six of us boys expressed to gether and we expressed it to Leander Smith and he is to devide it on each mans money to there parents or familys and you will probably have to recets to him for what money you get. The amount is thirty five dollars. The reason I expressed to him the balance of the boys wanted to sent to him and I thought I would send myne with theres because it would not cost as much. You will have to pay the express on what money you get for we could not pay the postage here. The agent did not know what it would cost each one will pay there amount of postage and you must pay him for his trouble. If he charges any thing probably you think I might have sent more money that I have but I want to get my likeness taken two or three times if I can. I want you to square up with Aunt Sarah McCord. Have the Mortgage all squared up so as the land will be free from all incumberence and I want you to keep it so as long as you can and then take good care of the balance of the money. Use what you are compelled to. You need not think by this that you are extravigant for I would not be afraid to trust you with five thousand dollars. I would feel as satisfied as though I had it in my pocket I have that much confidence in you that I can rest easy. I think you are a doing business as well as I could expect. I think I have the best womin in Iowa. I know one thing she is the nearest and dearest to me. I received your very kind letter the 22th inst. It was dated the 15th inst and I was very glad to heare that you was all well and on the land and amonge the living. You may think I am making light of such. I feel a little funny tonight. I have been to Pilot Knob today and just got back this Evening but I did not get drunk for I only had one dram to day and that was sweetened with water but that was the furtherest I have been from Camp without some Officer with me and I called it a bust (you would think so if you was kept clost as we have been for two or three month) for we could do as we pleased and that was a kind of rair thing. We are quartered at Iron Mountain six miles above Pilot Knob and the Railroad and it and it seems more like home that it has for the past few months. Threre is great curiosities in thispart of the country. The country we have marched over has been principaly Mountainous. This part here is is full of Iron. Iron is manufactured in to pigs here and at Pilot Knob. I will have to ajourn for the night fot it is geting late. I have boxed up a dress coat and a pair of gloves and a goald pen and a fiew other little trinkets all of which are in the coat pockets and one cap. They will be sent to oald man Randles. I put them in a box with Dave and Henry Perin. You will have to pay him the express and for his trouble. We are in an Iowa Brigade the 21th 22nd and the 23rd are in one Brigade. We are all here together and we do not know for certain where we will go but from all appearence we will go down the River. Today is the first of March and it is a very nice day. It is what we would call Spring wether in Iowa. O yes I had like to forgot to tell you what was the matter with me. I am so fat at the present that my bella nearly drags the ground. My bella sticks out so far fare that I can hardly see my feet. I am fatter now than I ever was in my life but there is nothing rong about that. If I could be so while I was in the Army I would be very thankful. I must close my letter by requesting you to write when ever you feel like it and I will write when ever you feel like it and I will write when ever I can. From you loving Husband Silas I Shearer to Elizabeth Shearer.

Camp High Ste Genevieve, Mo
Thursday March the 12th 1863

Beloved Wife It is the greatest of pleasure that I write you a few lines to let you know that I am well at the present time and I hope these few lines may find you all enjoying good health. I received you very kind letter the 8th inst which was dated the 4th inst and it was pleasure to me to hear from home and to heare that you were all well. I can rest easy as long as I can heare from you and that you all keep in good health. We left Iron Mountain the 9th inst and landed here the 11th inst. We have traveled over Mo a great deal but we never came acrost such roads as we did this last March. It was plank and gravel and lay through the richest of Mo that I have seen. The country is tolerable broken but I seen very good farms for a timbered country. It is settle principle by Dutch and French and you have an idea what kind of farmers they are. It has been a great country to make money. Everything that is raised can be sold for Cash and a very good price but the former part of our travels has been threw hollows and Mountains untill we came to west Plane which a a very nice country for this State but we did not stay there long and then we Struck back acrost the Mountains for the Railroad where we remained for several days and then we Struck for the River where we now lay for further orders. I cannot tell how long we will remain here probably not long. The reports are now that we are to reinforce Rosencrant in Tennessee. If that is the case we are not likely to stay here long. Without a doubt we are to godown the River soon and then it will be hard to tell what our destiny will be. This Brigade is said to be the Strongest one in the field. Is is composed by 21st 22nd and the 23rd Iowa Regts and the first Mo Battery and they are whole som boys. They think there is no such boys as the Iowa boys are the hang rite to gether and if it is the case in a battle they are a going to be hard to take if they have half of a chance and the right kind of a commander at the head of them. If our Colonel comes out cleare we will have a man that we can depend upon. Now I suppose you would like to know what is the matter with him. I will tell you something about it while was a Alton, Mo two companys of our Reg was sent back to Vanbeaurin and General Davidson ordered him to go with them and it is Ruleable for the Colonel to stay with the majority of the Reg so he ordered the Lieutenant Colonel to go withe them contrary to the Generals Orders and he arested him for it and he is now in St. Louis to be tried. I live in hopes that he will come out all rite and Strait. The reason I did not write such news before was because when we was down in MO our letters was opened by the head commanders of our division and if we wrot any thing concerning our movement or strength it was destroyed and I would not write much of anything. We had pretty hard times when we was down in Mo but I will not write anything concerning it and when I come home I will tell you all about it. Soldiers now have thirty days furlow five out of a hundred can go home at once. Three out of our Co has gon home. I do not know whether I will go home or not. I would like to se you all but it costs half fair but staying such a short time I would hate to leave. when you get that money and things that I sent to you I want you to write and let me know what allyou got. You said Pap wanted me to write concerning Negroism. I will write what I know about it. Write soon so no more at present time but remain your affectionate husband Silas I Shearer to Elizabeth J. Shearer.

Probably part of earlier letter
talks about his likeness and that was early on

Well my love I am agoing to send you my likeness this time. I got three taken and they are not very good I send one to my Mother and one to Rachel and the other one to Genna They cost me a Dollar a peace you can see how I look with my whiskers off and since I have got fat it may get dammaged before it gets home Well my darling I would like to see you once more and kiss those Sweet Lips that I used to Kiss and enjoy the pleasure that we once enjoyed together Those pleasures Seems Sweet to me yet it gives me a great deal of pleasure to think of the past. Well Jane I will have to go on guard tomorrow and while there I will think of the loved ones at home so no more Your loving husband S. I. Sheare to E. J. Shearer

New Madrid Madrid Co Mo
March the 17th 1863

Dear Companion It is with a degree of pleasure that I embrace the present opportunity of writing you a few lines to inform you of my health which is tolerable
good at the present time and I hope when these few lines arives athome the will
find you all enjoying good health and pleasure. We left St Genevieve on board
the Chouteau which was bound for New Madrid. We got on board of her the 14th
and we lay untill the next the morning the 15th inst and we started down the river
and we landed at Cape Gereadu and our Artillery was put off and we rounded in
at Cairo about dark and we lay there till one Oclock the next morning and we
plowed the river for this point which we made about 12 Oclock We past island
No 10 by the River. It is about Eight miles above here The Mississippi and Ohio
is tolerable full. a few miles before we came to the mouth of the Ohio the Mississippi was running over the bottoms. The Ohio River being so full was the cause
of it. The 38th Regt is here and they doant know beans about War. They have
never Marched five miles since they have been in the service. They opened there
eyes when we toted them what we have been threw. The inhabitants here are
principly Secefs and they done as they pleased with the 38th. They said the
women would run the boys off of the guard lines and the men whould Sauce them
and talked as they pleased to them but when the 23rd came they opened there
eyes. Our Boys whas all over the country and town before night and they would
do as they pleased and the Secefs could not help thereselves. I would like to see
the women run our boys. They would be very apt to get a bayonet stuck in them
where it would not hurt them very bad. From what I can hear the 23rd is the
hardest Reg out. They have got that name anyhow but we will have to knock
under to the first Nebraska for we was with them and we know that much. There
was a fleet of six boats here today and they said they was bound for Vixburgh.
The gunboat that was with them was in the fight at Memphis and at the fight
when the Arkansas run threw our fleet. She has two or three holes in her that the
Rebels put threw her but did not damage her. I could see wher the Musketry had
pepered her pretty well. We are a looking for a boat to take us down the River.
Probably we are to go to Vixburgh. The Rebbles are trying to get out and our men
drives them back but I am a feared they will get out. I am in hopes we can make
a clean sweep of that place but I am doubtful. I heard this Evening that they was
a vacuating Vixburgh. They have raised a flag of truce and the supposition is
they are leaving it. It is bad news. I think probably you do not think so but you
dont know anything about War. I know that by experience I hear that they was
seven thousand troops called from Memphis to Vixbergh. We may probably stop
there. I was out from Camp this Evening and I talked to three Negroes that was
plowing and they said there Master was as feard of the 23rd as I am of A Snake

and they said that when the news came for us to leave they had an idea that he was a seting in his house a claping his hands for joy. They said since we came the distance he would go out of dore would be to piss and then back in his den. If we had General Davidson with us he would have to prove him self a Union man or else he would go to St Louis. That was the principle we worked upon when we was a running threw MO. It has been a rite smart while since I have heard from you and probably it will be a considerable of a while before I will get a letter from you. When you write direct by the way of Cairo, Ill. Uncle Pery said I must tell the folk that he is well and I will just say the balance of the boys that are with us are well. The wether here is fine at this time. The Sun shines very warm and of a night it is tolerable coald. They are plowing for corn here. We are as low down as Tennessee. I believe thatis all I have to write for my pen is bad my ink is pale my love to you will never fail so no more at present but remains your affectionate husband Silas I Shearer to E. J. Shearer

Millicans Bend Louisiana
April the 11th 1863

Dear Companion It is once more with pleasure that I embrace the present opportunity of writing a few lines to let you know that I am well at the present time and Ihope these few lines may find you in good health and enjoying pleasure. I received three letters from you which was dated March the 8th 14th and 29th. They came to my hand the 9thinst and they gave me great pleasure to hear from you and to learn that you was all well. Nothing pleases me better than to hear such news but I did not get any satisfaction about them thing only that they had got threw safe but that was good news to me. Dave Perin just received a letter from his wife and it contained her likeness and the children also and He said that you have yourn and Denna takes also to send to me. I will be a looking for it every day untill it comes. I will have to be in a hurry with my writing for the orders is that we are to leave in the morning. I do not know where we are a goingtoo. The 18th Indiana Regt left his morning but we privates can not tell where we are a going too when we get to our Destination or get back I will write again and let you know what we went for and what we done. I think the Army at Vicksburg is a going to run a narrow risk of being captured from the appearence of the things at present and I think from the appearance of things at the present time that this War cannot last longer than Fall but that is my opinion on this thing. Deserters that comes from Vicksburg say the Rebels has nothing to eat but corn bread and beef and reports is that they are dying of so fast in Vicksburg that they can hardly get plank enough to Bury them decent that that is fastenr than our Army goes at the present time. It is said to be healihier here at the Present time than it has been for a long time. You seemed to be uneasy about me and the Smallpox. You need not trouble you self about that. I have been vaxinated and it worked well. some Doctors say that a person Vaxinated would never take them and if they do they will not have it bad. You also wrote to me how I must treat my self. That is Nothing wrong about that and when I had the Measles you wrote that I must drink warm tea. Now I will tell you what I know by Experience when I had the measles I used nothing but coald water and I knew others that used Ice Water and they got along a great deal better than them that used tea. If I would have to Doctor for the Measles I would not use nothing els but Ice Water but a person useing that dont want to use teas. I would not have believed it if I had not seen it tried. I cameoff picket this morning and I do not feel very much like writing at the present but will write soon again so no more at present but remains your affectionate Husband. Silas I Shearer to Elizabeth J. Shearer O Yes I like to forgot since your letters have taken a rest they stand up a great deal better and very much refrest.

The following letter was included on the same letter above.

Camp at Millicans Bend Louisiana
April the 1st 1863

Dearly beloved wife it is once more I embrace the present opportunity of writing you a few lines to let you know that I am well at the present time and I sincerily hope these few lines will find in the enjoyment of good health. I have not written to you since we left New Madrid and the reasons I will give to you after a while and I have not received a letter from you since we left Iron Mountain and I am anxious to hear from home. I would like to know whether you got the money and other things that I sent to you. I have an idea that mail will be very irregular here. a part of our Division has been here two or three weeks and have not seen any mail since they landed. Now I will give you a mear sketch of our travels since we left New Madrid. We left New Madrid the 22nd of March and we started for Memphis where we was to report and I seen Peach Trees in bloom the day we started and the timber began to look green and at the present time the woods is tolerable green. We landed at Memphis last Monday a week ago and we lay there untill Saturday the 28th and we was on board the boat very nigh ten days and we had a very hard time of it. We was like a lot of hogs. whennight came the boys began to hunt there nests. Some would crawl under the Boilers and some in some corner or other and them that could not get such places would sleep on the stone coal and you know what kind of a bed that would be and them that did not like such places could set up if they chosed. We was in two storms while we was onthe boat. The day we left Memphis it was very windy and the waves run high. The oald boat would creak and bend but she plowed her way threw without any damage and it being so windy and dark. A Saturday night we run to shore and

44

cast ancor and in the night a Storm came up and it blew us down the River in a lot of brush and Saplins (the River being very high overflowed the bottoms) and they got Steam up and kept her there untill morning and we went a head again. The River is so high that it is running all over creation pretty nigh if a person did not care what they said. We came acrost several of the Iowa Regt at Lake Providence and the thirteenth was one among them. I did not go to see them but some of our Boys went Simon Wodson and Tom Vanfielt came to our boat. They did not come aboard and I did not get to speak to them. I heard from all the boys that I knowed but Jake. Hafs the boys did not think to enquire for him. I did not get to see the 17th Regt from what I can learn the 17th and 10th and 12th with the muskets fleet threw the Yazean pass probably I will not get to see them at all. If you know where the 36th is and what company Uncle Andrew is in I want you to write and let me know. I havent heard of them since we left St. Louis. Troops are camped along the River for nigh a hundred this side of Vixburgh. We are in nine miles of Vixburg by about Seventeen by Water. We are in Grants Army the 21st, 22nd, 23rd Iowa 11th Wisconsin and an other Regt I do not know the name of and 8th 18th Ind the 33rd and 93 Ill and the first United States regulars constitues another Brigade and the above named Ten Regts constitues the 14th Division of the 13th United States Army Corps. I seen plantations as we came down the River that the buildings that was on it would make a good sized town in Iowa and all this belonged to one man and the Negro housed was a great deal better than a majority of the houses in Iowa. A great many of the boys would enquire what town that was and the reply would be it is a plantation. The plantation that we are camped upon is a very large one. The Propriator has about two hundred and fifty working Negros. He planted about tenhundred acres of corn last year which principle went to Vixburgh and about thirteen hundred acres of Cotton and I can not tell where that went to. Nelson arrived here today. He looks hartier than I haveseen him for over a year and I was glad to see him for he has been absent for a long time. I want you to write what Regt Bens brother is in and what Co and where they are at. You wrote to me once and burnt the letter (having no place to keep them) and I forgot what Regt you said he was in. I must bring my letter to a close so no more at present but remains your most affectionate and loving Husband. S. I. Shearer to E.J. Shearer
Not to give this slip to Aunt Sarah.

Well Jane you must not think hard of me for not writing to you. I know I have not done right in not writing you a letter. It has been a long time since I have written you a letter. I have been under the weather and have not felt like writing but I have not forgot you yet. I supposed you have heard of the Death of Uncle Andrew. I have not heard any of the particulars. It Seems as though mother has a hard life in the world and a great deal of trouble with it but this is a troublesom world for us all to make the best of it. I long to see the time when this War will come to a close and that we may all be permited to return home and live in peace. Once more I would be very glad to see you all. I am a going to try to come home after Vicksburg is taking if any posible chance but if the Lord is willing I am going to try to come home before many more month. It is a geting tolerable Sickly here now. I am in tolerable health at present but I hope these lines will find you all in good health. I must close. I have sent you twenty five dollars by the way of Leander Smith. It was expressed at Millicans Bend April the 25th and I have not heard whether you have got it or not. from your loving husband S. P. Shearer to E. J. Shearer

Millicans Bend Louisana
April the 11 AD 1863

Dear Father and Mother It is with the greatest of pleasure that I take the present opportunity of addressing a few lines to inform you that I landed safe to the Regt. But Camp life dont appear to agree with me. It took me down the first instance but I am geting better verye fast. I am so that I can set on my Ass and drink tea thats a good propspect its better. The Regiment has marching orders I dont know where they calculate to go. I herd heavy cannonading in the Directon of Richmond Lous this morning. I can hear the Cannons Belch at Vixburg Everyday But I dont that that there will be much firing soon. Their right of But? There will Be A Big fight before many months. Ithink Vixburg is bound to fall sooner or later. Our Division is Camped on a Plantation. The plantation was owned by A Rebel Colonel. He was killed in the Battle of Shilo. There is about 3000 A in the plantation I must bring my seribling to a close. write as soon as you can. No more at present.
I. W. Shenkle to B & E Shenkle   S. I. Shearer
(Lines and doodles under the signatures.)

Millican Bend Louisiana
April the 8th 1863

Dear Brother I write you a few lines in answer to them you write to me. I am well at present and I hope these few lines will find you all enjoying good. I will tell you something concerning the Rebles and other things that has hapened. We are close to Vicksburg and we can hear from them every day or two. Yesterday the Rebles had a fight within themselves. The Reble conscrips throwed down there arms and the remainder was a going to compell them to take up arms and fight. They took there arms and pitcht into the Rebles and killed a hundred and fifthy of them and spiked two of there guns. If such is the case it is good news to us. Now for something els one of our Captains went into Vicksburg and spied around two days and nights and came out again unhurt and with out suspiction. Now you wonder how he done that. One of the Rebles lieutenant got a pass and came out as a Spy and he gave himself up to our men and this Captain changed close with him and got his pass and went into Vicksburg. This Liet deserted the Reble Army he took that plan there is Deserters from the Rebles every day to our Army. There was a Grand Review today and I could se Soldiers it appeared as though there was no end to them. Two Company of the 3rd Illinois cavalry is in our Brigade. I will not write any more at present but remains your affectionate Brother. S. I. Shearer to J. W. Shenkle.

Youngs Point Louisana
May the 23rd 1863

Dear Companion it is once more that I take my pen and ink to inform you of my health which is tolerable good at present and I hope these few lines may find you all well. We have seen pretty hard times for for past four weeks and to day is a very glomy day to us and I expect much more to someof the other boys. I will tell you the reason I did not write before this. We have been traveling steady for four or five weeks and I lost my Knapsack and everything that was in it and I did not have anything to write with. I lost my Knapsack the first battle we got in to. You may think hard of me for so doing but you must excuse me for this time and I will try and write oftener. I must tell you something about our travels since we crost the river in to the Miss State. We crost the River the last day of April but before we crost we lay three or four miles above Grand Gulf. We had full view of the gun boat fight while hey as above the Batteries. So we marched below that evening and crost the River the next day befor ground gulf and then we marched out in the country a few miles and stoped and got something to eat. By this time it was

Sundown dark did not stop us we continued our March untill twelve OClock in the night when we run into the Rebels. We was in line when they opened their Battery on us (Our Brigade was in advance) we was ordered to fall down and they Shot and Shell passed over us thick as hail (Our Officers being unacquainted with the ground) we have to lay under there fire for several minutes untill they could find position for our Battery and then we was Marchedon a side hill out of danger of the shell were we lay untill morning. I never was so afritened in all my life as I was that night. We lay in the lane it seemed to me that I reached acrost the lane we had one man killed that night but the next morning I was as cool as a cucumber. After sun up a while we was ordered to pitch into the Rebls. We marched threw a cane brak in an opened field and the Rebles was in another cane brak and we opened on them. They wounded four of our Company in a short time. I was not in all day when Alvy Smith was wounded. I helped cary him of and did not go back. I was with Alvy when he died though I was in hotest part of it I only fired twelve rounds. Our Regiment made a charge on the crest works at Black River Bridge. Our Regitment was successful in takeing the works and about sixteen hundre prisioners but we lost a great many men in a short time. We lost about one hundred and tenty five or thirty men killed and wounded. we had three killed in our Co. and the 29th Memphis, Tenn. We came up the River with some prisioners. We have between three and four thousand. It takes three Regt the sice of the 23rd to guard them. You would not believe a Regt could decrease as fast as this one has in three weeks we number between two or three hundred able for duty. I will tell you some of the boys that was killed and wounded at Black River Bridge. Irvin Benson was killed, George Culver was wounded in the leg, Uncle Pery McCord was wounded in the leg and it had to be taken off. We left Youngs Point last Monday and they had been fighting Eighth days then and I cannot tell how much longer we will have to fight before we get it but we have it completely surrounde. I cannot tell whether we will go back from here or go further up the River. I seen Elias and Barty twice since we was below. They was in a fight at Jackson, Miss but neither one got hurt. I must bring my letter to a close. We are on a Boat and it is so crowded that I can hardly write. So no more at present but remains your loving husband Silas I. Shearer to Elizabeth J. Shearer

Youngs Point La
June the 4th 1863

Dear Companion It is again I write you a few lines to let you know that I am in tolerable good health at the present time and I hope when these few lines arives at your hand they will find you all well and in good Spirits. I received two letters from you yesterday. They ware dated May the 5th and 20th. This first mentioned letter contained your and Dennas likeness and I was well pleased with it. I can see that it you but Denna dont look natural. The boys say you nor him looks natural but however I am well pleased with it. I shall look back when on the main Back to my native isle And almost think I heare again Thy voice and view thy Smiles But many days may pass away Erect again Shall See Amid the young the fair the gay One who resembles thee Yet when the pensive thought shall dwell On some ideal maid Whome fancys pencil pictured well And touced with Softest Shade The image I shall Survey And pausing at the view Recall thy gentle Smiles and Say O, Such a one I Knew I was glad to hear that you was all well but I was sorrow to hear the Mother was sick but I am in hopes she will be well soon. I hardly know what to write for I wrote to you a few days ago. Our Regt went with prisioners up to Memphis and when our Regt started back I was on Shore and did not get to go with my Regt and I was there two days before I could get to follow the Regt. The 23rd was fired into twice while going down the River but now one hurt in the 23rd and when I came down the Boat I was on was fired into and two or three men wounded. This was done by guarilas. They are geting so they fire on every Boat that passes. This Vicksburg fight is going on yet this is the Seventeenth or Eighthteenth day since our troops attacked the Burg but I do not think it can last much longer. We have been fighting ever since the first day of May. There has been a great many men killed and wounded on boath sides. I have seen Elias and Barty twice since they came down here. Uncle Andrews Regt is at Helena Arkansas but I did not stop to see him. I have not seen Nelson since we left Perkings landing to cross the River to attact the Rebles. I heard that Uncle Pery and George Culver was geting along very well and I must tell you that Kitt Hayses intended Husband had his leg taken at Jackson Miss He was wounded in the Charge. He is in the same Co that Barty is in. I wrote to you once about Uncle Pery and George Culver being wounded. They was wounded in the Charge at Black River Bridge. You must not think hard of me for not writing oftener for we are porely situated for much business but I will write when ever I can So no more at present but remains your loving Husband Silas I. Shearer to Elizabeth J. Shearer Excuse my bad writing if you please. *Script Lines*

(Insert)
Well Jane I will write a little in answer to somethings you have wrote keep this to

youself Well in the first place I forgot to tell you that I am well and hearty as present hopeing these lines may find you well and hearty Well you wanted me to be careful and not lay on the Picture Well I had no inclination for laying on the picture but if it had been the one the picture was taken from I Shouldent wounder if Sombody would have been overlaid for a Short time but the picture I kept closed to my heart I felt as proud of that picture as though it was Gold I thought I never Seen any thing so Sweet as that picture was it would do me So much good to See you again and get a fiew Sweet Kisses from those Sweet lips for thats what they are Well Jane I must close we have to leave

Youres as ever Silas I Shearer to E. J. Shearer

Youngs Point
July the 4th 1863

Beloved wife I again write a few lines to let you know that I am in tolerable good health at present. I hope these few will find you all well. I received two letters from you one was dated June tenth and the other June the 17th and I was glad to hear that you ware all well. Nothing gives me more pleasure than to hear such news. I was glad to hear that the money I sent got threw safe. I had got very uneasy about it but I flinch before I was hurt but I thought if I lost twenty five dollars it would ruin me. I have not drawn any money since I sent that home If I had been with the Regt I could have drawn it but I do not care very much for it is not very safe to send money from here. I must tell you about Vicksburg but I suppose you will hear of it before this reaches you. Vicksburg is ourn at last. It was surrendered last night sometime. I have not heard any particulars about it. The Steamer John H. Dickey has just past up the the River with a dispatch for the Upper Country and if you are takeing papers you will hear the particulars of it surrender it is rejoiceing news to me and I suppose more so to the boys that was fighting them. If it was peace declared I could hardly hold my self. I heard we has lost two more boys out of our Company since they have went to Vicksburg but I did not learn who they were. Our Regt went in the fight at Millicans Bend with One Hundred and Forty men and about one half was killed and wounded. Four men out of Co K was killed dead and one died of a wound afterwards. I do not suppose that there is a hundred and fifty men able for service at the present time and will be less if we stay down here this Summer. I have not heard from Uncle Pery for a long time. If you hear any thing from him I want you to write how he is geting along. I have written to Lean Smith concerning Alvys death and his things and I also have written to Father and Mother about Nelson's Death. I receive a letter direct to him the same time I received youren and that was yesterday Evening and I opened it and read it. It was from Father and Mother. I would like to come home and see you but I can not tell when it will be. I am a going to stay on this Boat as long as I can. We will be apt to move to Vicksburg soon. I would like to se the place very much so no more at present from you loving husband Silas J. Shearer to E. J. Shearer Send me a postage stamp once and a while I can not get them here. 2 Sons dead - Simeon and Nelson.

Vicksburg Miss
August the 10th 1863

Dear Companion It is again I write you a few lines to let you know that I am in tolerable good health at the present time and I hope these fiew lines may find you all well. I am with the Regt at present. I will send you thirty five dollars by our first Lietenant to Marshalltown and he will put it in the Office and Start it for Edenville. I will not writ any more at present. I will write again in a day or two. Writ when ever you can so no more at present yours as ever
Silas I. Shearer to Elizabeth J. Shearer

Vicksburg Miss
August the 10th 1863

Dear Companion I will now try and write you a letter that is a few more lines that I wrote a fiew minutes ago concerning the money I sent you for I was in a big hurry to get it ready. Now I will tell you how much I sent and who I sent it by. Our First Lieutenant is a going to start home in an hour or two and I thought it would as safe with him as it would to be expressed from here and he is to putt it in the Office at Marshalltown and you will receive it at Edenville. I send you a twenty dollar bill a ten an a five all amounting to Thirty Five Dollars. I could send you more money but you are not needing it and there is chances for speculation down here if a person has money. You may think I want to spend money foolishly. Well a person is more apt to spend money when they have considerable. Now I will tell you how much money I drew. I drew fifty two dollars. If you can loan your money at intrust to some one that is good and can get good Security I think it would as good as you could dowith it. What money you doant want to use is dead property for it Eats nothing or brings in nothing that is while you have it rapt up and put away in some drawer or other for fear a Dollar would get away and you would not know it. Now you can do as you please as far as the money is concerned but do the best you can with it. You can tell how things runs in Iowa and whether it would be safe to loan it or not. Now I must tell you something about Vicksburg. I suppose you have heard and read a great deal about our Mortars that was a tareing the place all to pieces and killing all the people that was in it. I do not believe them Mortars done five hundred Dollars Damage to the town. It was only once and a while that a house was Struck with them but in traveling over the town a person would be asked every once and a while what made that hole in the ground. The answer would be a Mortor Shell done that. The Small Guns done a great deal the most damage to the town and people and you heard conciderable about them. Batteries that our men had placed to throw hot shot in town to burn it up. When we got down here we could not see nor hear nothing of such a Battery. and that Canall what a great thing that was. I have seen that Canall. Some places it is ten or fifteen feet deep and it would very from that to three feet. When I seen it it was dry and the water in the river lacked eight or ten feet of being up to the canall. That is the way the papers lies about a great many things. Now I will give you the price of some produce and what we have to pay for it when we buy it. Potatoes are from Seven to to Nine Dollars per BBL We can get a four pint tin full for Twenty or Thirty Cts and green apples from five cts a piece or forty or fifty cts a dozen and peaches fifteen to twenty five cts per doz and tolerable good sliced Onion is worth five cts a piece. Now you can see the contrast between this and Iowa.

Vicksburg
August the 11th 1863

I received your very kind letter yesterday dated the 22nd and I was golad to hear that you were all weell but was sorrow to hear of the bad luck among the connection. You wanted to know what time Nelson died. I cannot give you the exact time though he died between three and four Oclock in the Evening. Your Mother wanted to know whether he had drawn any new clothing. He has not drawn any thing since he left Demoin except one pair of shoes. His dress coat was all that was of any account and that was left in his Knapsack and was given to the Commander and I do not know his name. I think it will be doubtful whether they every get it or not. If I had been well I would have taken care of his coat but as it was I could not. The coat was not soiled a particle. I seen Luther Randles yesterday evening. He was just from St. Louis and he seen Colson and Uncle Pery. He said Uncle Perys leg was almost well and Colson was about the oald fashion. I am with the Regt now we have eight or nine men able for duty at present. We have had thirty three men killed died and discharged that is Co K six or eight only has been discharged. You need not send me any stamps for I can buy them here so I must close. I hope this will find you in good health. Yours as ever S. I. Shearer to E. J. Shearer Oh yes Wattermeleons sells from 75 cts tothree dollars a piece thatsall.

Carlton LA
August the 18th 1863

Dear Companion It is again I write you a few lines to let you know where we are and how I am geting a long. My health is tolerable good at present and I hope these few lines may find you all enjoying good health and pleasure. I have not received a letter from you for some time but we are a great ways apart and I cannot expect a letter every week. We are six miles above New Orleans I dont think we will remain here long. I think from the appearance of things that we are to go to Mobeal Al soon. I expect we will go around by water. It seems as though the Western Army has all the hard work to do but a few more hard Battles and it will be plaid out unless recruited. I do not pretend to say the the Rebs can stand a siege. The best for their Army was as badly used up as ours was but such a siege as Vicksburg is death on boath Armies. When we passed Port Hudson I was surprised to see such a looking place. I did not see any town whatever and to look at the place looked like it was of no account to us or the Rebs. We did not stop at the place so I could not tell much about it. Dry goods and fishes of all discription are tolerable cheap. I want you to write to me when you get that money I sent you. I want to know what that token was that you folks had before Nelson died. So no more at present. yours as every S.P. Shearer to E. J. Shearer

Carrollton LA
August the 27 1863

Dear Companion Yours of the twenty seventh came to my hand the twenty fift inst and it was read with pleasure. I was glad to hear from you and to hear that you were all well. Nothing gives me more pleasure than to hear such. Health is the formost thing in life without it there is but very little pleasure and what is a person unless they can enjoy some pleasure. They are one of the most miserable creatures living. I am in tolerable good health at the present time and I hope these few lines may find you all enjoying good health and pleasure. We have one of the most beautiful camps I ever seen. It is as nice an green as ever you seen on the Iowa Prairie. Although it is level it is nice and dry and has the appearance of a healty place. It is kept very clean the boys and girls gathers up all the trash and stuff this is thrown away by the Soldiers and that keeps all the filth away. Citizens say it is very healthy here at Carrollton. They say it is a great deal healther than it is at the City. I would rather live here than any place I have seen this side of Keokuk. We have a breeze here all the time which makes it very pleasant. It is tolerable cool her of a night. I can bear a blanket most very night. It is not as warm here of a night as it is in Iowa. You talk a great deal about furloughs if you knowed as much about furloughs as I do you wouldnt write so much about it. Furloughs are hard to get when I can get a furlough I will come home and see you all but the boys from our corner will not get to go home. All the Balence does. If I must say it you and Bill Thompson Wife are considerable alike always Ding Donging to come home on a furlough. I would like to come home and want to go as bad as you want me to come. You need not take any offence at this I thought I would let you know that furloughs cannot be had when ever a person wanted one. I want you to write to me about the Draft in Iowa whether they are doing anything with it and how the people Stand it and whether Jake Crouch has an notion of War yet and how they are geting along by this time and whether Turner has the Rheumatse yet. I would be glad if this War was over with so as we could all go home. From the appearance of things at present I cannot set how it can last much longer. Where the Rebles have been enforcing there Conscript law Citizens have been excapeing it as much as possible. There was Seventeen or Eighteen Deserters here from Mobeal. They are deserting every point as much as posible. I must quit my Scribling for you will not believe half I have writen So no more at present from your loveing Husband Silas I. Shearer to Elizabeth J. Shearer.

Camp at Brashear City La
Sept the 17th 1863

Dear Companion It is once more that I embrace the present opportunity of adressing a few lines to you to let you know where we are and how I am geting along. My health is not very good at present although I am geting better. I had the flux since we came down here is the cause of my health being bad. I hope these few lines will fin you all enjoying good health and pleasure. We are at the present Eightymiles West of New Orleans on the Opoloosa Rail Road. If you had a war map you could see where we are. This is one of the porest countries I ever seen. It is a very Swampy Country we have very poor water to drink and hardly enough of that for the water that is in the Bayous are salty. The tied runs up of a night between Eighteen to Thirty inches So you may know that we are tolerable neigh to the Gulf. I would not be surprised if we took a Scout threw Texas but we will have to fight before we go far. The Rebs are fortified about Seven miles from here. They are on an Island and I should not wounder if they would be gobled up for they have no way of retreating and more than that they have a lot of Conscrips and they have to guard them to keep them from Deserting. An Army of that kind will not do much at fighting. Although they are under oald Zack Taylors Son and if takes after his oald Dad he will be a hard nut to crack. Reble prisoners say that conscrips does themmore harm than good. They can not trust them to anything. We are geting considerable of a force here and troops coming in all the while that is what makes me think they will be gobled but I may be mistaken but I hope not. I can not see for my part how Rebel troops can last much longer. My opinion is that South Carolina will be the first State back in the Union. My reasons is this Charleston is all the place in the State to amount to any thing and when that falls it will be very nigh rid of Rebs and so there will be nothing to keep it out of the union. It beingthe First State Out will be the first in and then the balance of the States will follow. You may think I am foolish in thinking so but I have a rite to my ideas as have all the balance of the people. I have writen enough about this. I have received two letters from you and this is the answer to them. I was glad to hear from you and to hear you were all well. The reason I have not writen to you before was this. We was ordered to leave our Knapsack and I left my paper in it So I had nothing to write a ltter on and I fear we will never see them a gain. I have an idea that my letters will be few and scattering for a while but you must not be uneasy if you do not get a letter for a month or two. I will write when ever I can. I do not want you to stop writing because I have to. It is not my wish to stop writing Somethings a person is compelled to so I would like to be at home so as I could help tend the farm next year and I hope I will be writ and give me all the particulars of the day and how thepeople are geting along and where Joe Williams is and how he is geting along. I would like to heare from all the neighbors. I must close so no more at present from your loving Husband Silas I Shearer to E. J. Shearer.

Camp at Brashear City La
Sept the 22nd 1863

Dear Companion. It is with pleasure that I embrace the present opportunity of addressing you a few lines and I am happy to say that I am well at present and hope I will remain so. I sincerely hope these lines will find you all enjoying good health and pleasure. I received a letter from you of the Second inst. It came to hand the Twentieth inst and it gave a great satisfaction to hear that you were all well. That is the first thing that attacts my attention. The question is when I see a letter are they all well when I find they are then I am satisfied. The wether is fine (you might ask how is the Ewe if the wether is so fine) with the exception of the night which is tolerable cold The way we are prepared to sleep we have no woolen Blankets with us A gum blanket is all we have to keep warm and they are like ice of a coald night and the fire of a hot day. Our shelter from the Storms (is what we call Dog Tents) Shelter tents I will describe them as nigh as I can It is a peace of Trilling about six feet square and them that wants one of those tents has to lug it on his back or any other way he can get along with it So he toats it (as the

Negro says). It is intended for two soldiers to bunk together and when night comes they will fasten there tents together and Stretch it a crost a pole and fasten the four corners to the Earth Boath ends of the tent are left open so as the wind and storm can blow threw them without any dificulty whatever for it is only six feet three it. Henry Perin and myself are two dogs that occupies one of those kennels. Our Brigade occupies those kinde of tents and they make a very nice dog town. Since we left Vicksburg we have a camp gaard while we was at Carrollton there was a camp called for and Col Glasco Sayes God-dam it this Brigade want guard itself. I have known them to detail a guard out of another Brigade to guard us when ever our boys are on guard and other ones wants to go out they will turn there backs and swear they never seen them. That is the kind of boys we have in our Brigade. We have thirteen men in our Company with the Ordly Sargent and he is in command at the present time. I and Henry Perin Downes and Summers is all theones from Edenville (Rhodes) that is with the Company. We have between one hundred and fifty and two hundred men in the Regt at present it looks small to what it did at Burnside I was glad to hear that you was at that great Speaking at Peora and that you was well pleased. I would like to have been there to heard it but from what you say whether I would have liked the Speaches or not is unknown to me. If they were not Union men I could have swallowed there Doctrin for I am a Union man and will not support any man this is not for the Union. All men that is not for the Union is against it and such is worse that Rebels in arms against us and we are into it now and we can fight them in the North as well as in the South but I am in hopes we will have no such things as that to do. You to say about the Negros as far as that is concerned I have nothing much to say for my eyes dont see as they did when I left home. Since I have got down here and seen what Slavery was and where it had run to it changed me in a political since of view Slavery is what caused this War and the Principle of it has changed me considerable. I have had prisenors to tell me that it made no difference how much a man was worth He was nothing thought of unless he owned a Negro or two and a poor man was not as much thaught of as a Negro and I think the best thing we can do is to wipe Slavery out but do not think it will be done at present but I do not think we will have Slavery directly but indirectly I think it will be a gradual emancipation and what will be fit for the Army will be put init. They are just as good Soldiers as theWhites They look like men when uniformed of I have seen Regt with commissioned officers of there own coler and they looked Sniptious. Those men North that is So bitterly opposed to the emancipation of Slavery had serve as long a time in the South as I have There ideas would change two you people North reading knowes nothing about such things without experience. Experience teaches a dear School but fools will learn in no other and the South is begining to find it out. Takeing the Negros from the South and arming them is one of the greatest blowes that was Struck. To put this rebellion down you people North may not see it but I see it here very plane. Now you may take me to be an abolitionist but that matters nothing. I am a War Democrat and you may call them what you please So no more at present your loving husband Silas I. Shearer to Elizabeth J. Shearer.

October the 3rd 1863
Dear Daughter

I take the present opportunity to write you a fiew lines to let you know that we are all well at present I got your letter some time a go and was glad to hear that you was well. I did not answer your letter rite away I heard that Elias and Barteny had got back to they ware both well I heard frome Andy last week he was not very well he had ben to the doctor Our wheats crops was no a count. and it was so dry that is kept the corn back and then this fall the frost come and killed it all. I have bought the West part of the old place and I expect to move in about 2 or 3 weeks I that that I could be better satisfied after I got back on the old place I got a letter from Pery and I wrote up to him to know hom I couldt do up there and he never rote to me and I could not wait any longer for the place was about to be sold. I have sold most of my stock I hant got much to write for I have got so many letters to rite but from Catherine Shearer to Elizabeth Jan Shearer Write soon dont forget it

Vermillion Bayough LA
October the 20th 1863

Dear Companion It is again I write you a few lines wich will be in answer to letters I received from you I received two of them yesterday and one Some Two or Three weeks ago and I was glad to hear that you were all well. I am so fat and hearty as I ever was in my lifee I am geting so fat that they Boys laugh at me and tell me I have put myself to a Negro wench which causes me to improve so fast. If that is the cause it is very good medicine I hope these few lines will you all enjoying good health and pleasure. You seem to think that Gen Grant dont use us rite but you see different to what we do. We are at the present detached to General Bankes Army and the boys wish that Gen Grant was in command. They think they would fair better Gen Banks is very Strict. We are geting down towards Texas but whether we will go in to Texas is more than I can tell. Some say we will go to Brownsville on the RioGrande That is closet to Galverston where the South goes out and in to do there traiding with foren Nations but they say we will have to fight the Women before we can get in to Texas. If that was all we had to fight it would be fun for us. We would take them by the point of Bayonet which is the quickest way of fighting. I was glad to hear that you had visitors to see you from Indiana. I would like to been at home to seen them. I suppose there was great rejoiceing when your Granpap came to see you. I know it was great pleasure to you to see those folks. You had not seen for years and did not know whether you ever would see them again. Such things will revive a person a great deal I know that by Experience when my oald friends comes to see me here in the Army I feel rejoiced to see them. It revives me very much. This is one of the pretiest countries I ever seen as we march along I can see peach trees in blossom and plum trees thinks they will not be behind there neighbour peach So they show there white and most delicate bloom as they think and other blossoms that I could mention which is very uncommon in the North. The weather is fine here with the Exception of the night which is tolerable cool and makes it very dis-agreeable to us for we are not prepared for cold weather but we have to get along the best way we know how. most of the boys have nothing but gum blankets and it is like sleeping between ice and is very disagreeable sleeping in such a Bed. We was paid two months pay a couple of weeks ago and be down here where it is not very safe to send money home. I did not send any So I loned fifteen dollars to one of the boys and I have the same amount in my pocket. I have know twenty dollars loned out. Whether I ever get it or not. If you can buy that Fallish Forty that lays west of my land I want you to get it if you can get it at any reasonable price That is what I am fishing after but you need not let every boddy know it or it may be hard to get. I am cooking for the Company and I baked some cornbread for dinner. I have got so I can bake very good bread I think by the time I serve my time out you will be know where with me in the cooking line You must excuse me for not writing ofterner. It is only once and a while that we can send a letter I do not know when I can send this one but I thought I would have it ready Yours as every S. I. Shearer to E. J. Shearer

Camp Nigh New Iberia LA
November the 2nd 1863

Dear Companion It is again that I take the opportunity of writing you a few lines to let you know how I am geting along and where we are. I am enjoying good health at this time and I sincerely hope these few lines will find you all Enjoying good health and pleasure. I received a letter from you a few days ago and was glad to hear that you were all well but was sorrow tohear that you and Mrs. Ben could not agree on Political and I am sorrow tohear that she holds me as a Traitor to my Country. I dont know what I have done that she can call me Such. I have done all that I can for my Country if that be but little it is a great deal more that (what she would call) her own Patriot that stays at home with the Excuse that he would come if he could leave his family. How many thousand have left there familys and home for there purpose of fighting for there Government and to maintain the Union but such men (in her estimation) are Traitors because they have the name of A Democrat. Just look at the thing it is enough to discourage the Soldiers that are fighting for there Country. There is a great many of the Soldiers that are Democrats and if they are Traitors they would not be worth any thing to the United States but you may ask any Republican that has been in the Army and if they say that Democrats are not as good and true in the fields then I will treat. As for the Cow you can do asyou please with her for you are there to tend to the things So use your own pleasure about it. Since I have written the last letter to you we have maid a two days March Northwestward and laid two or three day clost to Opaloosa and then we took our back tract and marched three days and now we are in camped at a very nice place. Sometimes Revelee would beat at three and march at five and rain sometimes all day and it was prety hard on us. I would have to be up until ten or Eleven Oclock a cooking and then be up at Revelee in order that we could be ready to march at the set time. Where we are to go from here is more than I can tell. Probably I can tell better in the next letter. Some say we are to go to New Orleans and take a vessel and go by water to Texas and some say to Mobeal and others to Tennessee and the Remainder say that we are to go back toward Opoloosa One or other of these places will undoubtly be our destination. Well Jane this is the 3rd day and I will write a few lines more. We have nice wether here the majority of the time and the bad wether is when we have to march which makes it very disagreeable at that time but when we get in Camp and get dry we forget the hardship we have to encounter withe the indication of this country is healthy with the Exception of one thing and that is Water. The Water that is used here by the Citizens is Cistern water but we do not get but a very little of that. Still the Water we use now does very well. It is a great deal beter than we have used and probably better that we will have to use. I have seen Cottonwood trees a budding before the green leaves were all off and gardens of all discription Garden that every thing was ripe and gardens that was about half ripe and some that was just planted. A person can have a green garden here all the while. A person can raise any thing here except wheat. I have not seen any of that yet. There's some of the pretiest trees here that I ever seen. The name of these trees are live Oak and they are litterly covered with Spanish Moss. This Spanish Moss is used for Buggy Seats and Cushions. There is a great Many curiosities to be seen in this part of the Country. It pays a person for seeing this part of the Country. If they did not have to stay so long for my part I have stayed long enough and would like to be at home with my family. I long to see the end of this War when we can all go home and live in peace once more. I will close for this time. My respects to all. I would like to see you all but it would not pay for me to go from here. Yours as every S. I. Shearer to E. J. Shearer

Camp Berwick Bay LA
November the 11th 1863

Dear Companion I take this afternoon as an opportunity of writing you a few lines which will be in answer to a letter just received from you It was wellcomly received and gladly read It is pleasure to me to hear that the friends I left behind calls me a Traitor and further more that I was scared into it. I think such people have but very little sympathy for Soldiers and Soldiers wives. Such folks that are a feared to go to War should be glad that somebody was Sceared into it. It would be a very fine thing if they was less volunteering and more Drafting. Then we would get some of these brave men that stayes at home and sayes dont we give the Rebles fits. We are driving them from every point here lately and we can whip them and we will whip them and then after they say all of this Step up to them and say Brother Union man less volunteer what say you What would the answer be. Why it would be this I can not leave my family they would all Starve and Freeze to Death in the winter. I think it would look well in such men that wants to stay at home to say but very little and mind there own business and let men that are a fighting for there Country alone. If they will wait untill I get home then I am ready to be called a Traitor by those men. If those men was here and went threw the hardships that we have then they would see where traitorism was They would be the first men to grumble It is always the case but they are at home enjoying comforts of life and all they have to do is to blow about the true men of there country. While we are here agoing threw hard ships and trials and take it all with good cheer and when ever any good news comes from home concerning Unionism the boys will raise the Yell and still they are traitors among them. It almost makes me mad to think such men are left at home. I am down on Copper Heads and Traitors are hard as anyboddy and so it all Soldiers that I ever seen. I am for the union and let slavry go up or down. We have to be ruled by the President and let us get as clost to gether as possible and we will thrive and do well and finly succeed in puting down the rebellion. It is enough on this subject.

We have made some pretty hard marches since we have been down here. We have been down to Opaloosa and got back to Brasher City or oposite acrost the Bay. We maid a two day force march a coming back. While we was lying at New Iberia the Rebls maid a dash on the third and fourth division for our Army Corps and took several Prisonors but did not kill many and the news came that the Rebls was a going to make a dash on the town where we lay. So we was ordered to march at three OClock. So we marched about four miles to the forkes of a road where we lay in line of Battle untill about noon and know Rebles came and we was ordered in to camp and the next morning Early as common the 11th Wis was ordered in to line of Battle untill daylight and the morning following we was done likewise and at five we struck out for Brashear. Our Division was all that was here when the 3rd and 4th Division was attacked. They was two days behind us. The news is that they captured nigh a brigade of our men but our men held them and the Rebles retreated the engagement was but short. The news is now that we are to go around by water to Brownsville on the RioGrand We hear that the second division of our Corps is there. If we do go there we will not hear from one another once in two months. If it wasint for crossing the waters I would as soon go there as anyplace. I am well harty and fat as ever I believe I am fatter than I ever have been in my life. I hope these lines will find you all enjoying good health and pleasure. I believe I have writen all I can at present so no more at present from your loving Husband Silas I. Shearer to Elizabeth J. Shearer. P.S. Well Jane you may send me a Stamp once and a while for I am where I can not get them.

Ft. Esperenza Matigorda Island December the 19th 1863

Well Jane I suppose you think I have forgot to write to you or probably you may think I have forgoten you but you need not think so for I have forgoten neither you nor forgoten to write to you. It has been a month or more since I have written you a letter and I will tell you the cause of it by and by. Well Jane my love I will let know how I am geting along in the way of health. I am fat and hardy as a buck and have been for the last two or three months. I have an idea I would weigh nigh on to two hundred. The boys are generaly healthy here I trust these lines will find you all enjoying good health and pleasure. I have received two letters from you since we have been here and this will serve as an answer to boath of them. I was sorrow to hear that the Babe had burnt herself but I am in hopes she is well by this time. Well Jane now I must tell you something about our travels. Since we left Berwick (where I wrote my last letter) we was ordered to report at Algears (Oposite New Orleans) So we got a board the cars at Brashears and run to the above named place where we lay a day or two and then embarked for the Rio Grand and when we got there was was ordered to report at Mustang Island. Two Maine Regt and the 19th and 20th Iowa and a part of the first Brigade had already been there and taken a fort and all that was in it (a part of the first Brigade was with us). We ancored at the Mouth of the Riogrand in Site of Mexico. A part of one night we would have went to Brownsville had it not been so easy taken but our forces had possession of it before we got there. We embarked the 15th and landed the 21th We got on the Boat in the Evening and run down to the mouth of the River that night and ancored untill morning and then we struck out in to the mighty Deep. It was a very beautiful day every thing looked beautiful but in the Evening behold a cloud appeared. I says Downs look at that cloud we are a going to have a wind

Downs said he thought not but when morning came the wind was blowing and kept increasing and the night following it clouded up and it commenced raining and storming and then we had a nice time (if a fellow dont care what he says) I was sick the first day the wind blew and I vomited like a dog but the vomiting only lasted about a day and the vessel was pitching around considerable but the next two days was the blunt. We had know place to stay only out in the rain and storm. Some of the boys went down into the hole among the Mules and Horses. I was sick all the while on board and I could not stand it down there for I had to have fresh air. By this time the Boat was rocking from side of side and then she would pitch into a wave as though She was Mad and Every now and then a wave would was over the Decks where we was and we was wet all the while. One Morning we was lying on Deck and I was lying by a Cannon and a wave run over the deck about three feet and washed the decks very nigh clean. It broke one end of Cannon loos that I was by and smashed my fingers for me and washed me about ten feet in under another Cannon where I caught. I was all under Water and it washed a man in our Company and Barrel down the hole but it did not hurt him. There was several men washed overboard but only one out of our Regt. I get tired of such Soldering I wisht I was at home with Jane. A great many of the boys was Sceart some would grunt whenever the Boat would turn on her side and other ones would say O she cant stand it much longer we will all be drowned in the Gulf but I was not much frighted for I was so sick that I did not care very much. She would sink or swim sometimes She would be away on the waves so that a person would have to look away down to see the water and sometimes and sometimes the waves would be like mountains above us and for all that it was know Storm to what some Storms are on the Gulf but wasent I a proud bird when I got on shore. The ground I walked on would rock as did the vessel. I would rather soldier by land than by water. We landed on St Joe Island and we marched to a bayou and then we crost over on this Island (the name of which is Matigordia) and we marched two or three days and came to above named Fort which was garrisoned by the Rebs which was between Six or Seven Hundred strong. The Evening we got here it stormed so we laid inline of battle for a day or two and it got so cold that it frose ice and inch and a half thick. Our cannon was very small compared with theres but was like Bulldogs They would stand there ground and bark severly. The Rebs had Eight guns in this Fort. Four 24 pounder and two 20 pounder and one 1.28 pounder but they did not hurt any of our guns. Our Regt was about two miles from the Fort as a reserve (being all the Regt of our Brigade here) and we had a Battery planted in front of us and a little to the right. When ever the Rebs would fire there big gun at the Battery the balls would come bounding down toward our Regt but we had no man hurt in our own Regt our little Army lost one man and nine wounded. most of the men was hurt of the Explosion of the Magazines which the Rebs set fire too when they evacuated. We was in a hundred and fifty yards of the Fort when one exploded but no one was hurt at that time. The Rebs had a Fort with one gun about two miles and a half from this to cover there retreat. We got five or six prisioners and they say they lost but one man. I understand that no more fighting is to be don in Texas for Thirty days. The Governor wants to surrender the State and all the troops that he enlisted. Our Army has raised three Regt since they have been at Brownsville. The prisioners say one half of the people in Texas are Union men they say we will not have to do much fighting in Texas. Our Regt. is to garison this Fort We was lucky Dogs by being sent to Texas. If we had not come here we would have been sent to Tennessee. I understand that the Division that Elias and Barty in was in the last Fight that Grant had. Now I must tell you an andecdote that occured between Grant and Banks at Carrollton. When we was out on General Review (Grant came down to see the 13th A C before he left) and after review General Banks says to General Grant I dont like those men of yours. They have not got Style enough about them. Grant says well General by God if you do not like these men I will take them back. They was not drilled for Style they were drilled to fight and by God they will do it they know how to fight. Banks excepted the men and said nothing more about it. If you can read this you can do more than I can so no more in this From your husband Silas I. Shearer to Elizabeth J. Shearer

Fort Esperenza, Texas
December the 30th 1863

Dear Companion This Evening gives me the opportunity of writing a few lines which will be an answer to a letter just received from you. It came to me last Evening and I felt rejoiced to think I had the pleasure of reading another letter that was writen by you. I was glad to heare from all of you but was sorrow to hear that you were not well but I hope ere this reaches you that you will be Stout and harty again. I am fat and hearty as a buck and enjoying Soldiers life the best I know how which is hard at the best. I hope these few lines will find all of you Enjoying good health You write that the health of the Country is not very good I am sorrow to heare of such news It keeps me uneasy all the time. You wrote that there had not been no Deaths Since you wrote last week. I have not got that letter yet so I am left in the Dark. It appears as though some Deaths has occured in the Neighborhood. I feel proud to hear that Pa is doing so well for he has had considerable of bad luck since he cam to Iowa but I hope he will have better luck from this on. It pleases me very much to heare of the folks a doing well in Iowa. Whenever it raines So ofs my Dish is upside down (but it is would rain Shit my Dish would be heaping full a runing over) you need not read this if you delicate about it. I will mark it so as you can tell when it is and you can skip over it if you wish. *(Wavy lines)* I would like to be at home with you and hear the cars whistle if I have good luck and plenty of it I can ride home on the cars and I hope that will be soon. And I think probably if nothing hapens more serious than has for the last six months it will not be long. You hoot at this and think I am foolish for thinking so perhaps I am but I can not see it at present. It is a great deal better for a person to live in hopes If he Dies in Dispare if Soldiers thought they would never get home Wyn they would be the most miserablest creatures on the face of the Earth. You need not fret youself about me when every you heare of a Battle. You should think of the approaching end of War which most ashurdly will come Sooner or latter. You should rejoice in the place of morne if you do Either one for a troubled mind is hard on the Constitution and will Eventualy bring on Disease. So do not trouble youself about me for I will do the best I can. The prisioners say we will not have very much fighting to do in Texas. They say that there is about six or Eight Thousand Enlisted troops in Texas the blance are all Conscripts and they wont fight for a grate many of them are Union men. A lieutenant and a lot of his men cam in to our lines and gave themselves up (This Lieut was an Enlisted man) he said the Rebs was about to conscript him so he Enlisted with the determination of coming in to our lines the first opportunity. This is the fact for he was in the Fort guarded by our Boys and he further says that he knows of Companys and there commanders waiting for the opportunity of steping acrost the line. They say if the Army of Texas knew what we was fighting for they would lay down there Arms before they would have the State invaded. The Rebels dread the Texicans that will come in to our lines more than they do us Yankees as the call us. Our men had a little Skirmising to do. Our men captured one or two Rebs the other day and sent them to the Fort The Rebs are a fortifying against us on a narrow neck of land thinking they can keep us back by so doing but I rather think they will have to evacuate that place before many weeks or Els they will have to whip us or Surrender. I suppose from accounts we can land a force in the rear of them. Reports say that General McGrouder is concentrating his forces at this place in order to drive us back. Well Jane I will have to say goodnight for it is after tattooo *(Wavy Lines)* Well Jane this is the third day of January and I will have to write some more for I have received the letter that left me in the Dark. It was written December the Second and it came to me January the first and I was pleased with it although I had read a letter of later date from you. I am glad of the chance of reading oald letters. It seems as though letters comes very slow from you but I presume that is not your falt. Well Jane I will tell you the reason which I did not finish my letter before this. I suppose you have heard considerable about these Texicans Northerners I have got consideraly acquainted with them Since I came here. The night I commensed this letter it was very warm So I striped off pretty well to go to bed and a person could hardly sleep with close over them. It was warm until 11 OClock in the night the wind shifted to the North and it came with a tremedious blast and then it was coald enough to freeze a person immediately and it blew our tent to the ground but we pulled it over us and lay there till morning and we got up to Enjoy the pleasure of a disagreeable day and it bliew that day and the next night and then ceased and the way I can describ the camps to you is to look at a peace of timber after a Herikane goes threw it. The tents was blowen down and strewed in every direction it reminded me of a deserted Cesesh (Seacoast) Town. I wisht then I was at home. We have had several of those Northeners but none as hard as this last one was when ever we have one of those fellows the Sand runs like the Snow does in Iowa of a coald winter day. Now I will tell you how we get water to use Well in the beginns I will just say the Sand drifts here in heaps like the Snow in Iowa and we have to dig in these sand banks to get fresh water. The higher the Bank is the Better the Water is and we have to dig from three to six feet deep. If we dig two deep we get salt water and sometimes if we dig a rod from the Springs we get Salt wateer These Sand Banks that we get water out of is on the Beach and to go out back of the Sand Bank from the Beach and dig we get Salt water just as Salt as it is in the Ochean. Well Jenna we are still guarding this fort and I understand the Col n is a going to try to stay here our time out if there is any posible chance. It is a very disagreeable place to stay at but it is better than Marching The 23rd cant expect to get a better place than this. I am satisfied to stay here Well Jenna I got a letter from Mother the other day and they were all well and she said my Brothers was well the last time she heard from them. I expect Elias and Barty was in that fight that General Grant had The news is here that a part of the fifth Iowan as taken Prisioners and they were all in one Division. If you know how they got threw or anything about the fifth I want you to let me know it. Well Jane you need not bother yourself about that piece of land for land will be a great deal cheaper after this War ends then what it is now. Jane I want you to send me some Stamps for it is imposible to get them here. With these fiew lines I will have to close O Yes I like to for got to tell you I brought your likeness safe across the waters with me and it was dipt under more than once The Case got spoilt of course Tell Denna that his likeness crost the waters with his Pa So no more at present yours as every S. I. Shearer to E. J. Shearer

January 1864

Well Jane this is the Eight of January and my letter not finished yet and the reason is this it has been So cold for the past week that I could not finish the letter and if it had been finished I could not have sent it for the Sea has been so rough that there has not been no boats in so we could Send mail and since I have begun writing I will just say that I am well and hearty and hope these will find all of you well and hearty. Well Jane I received a letter from Elias today and it was Sorrowfull news to me It announced the Death of Barty and George M. Shearer it appears as though my Brothers has bad luck he has faught the Rebs at a great many places and was wounded once from all accounts he was a Brave Soldier there Devis

made a charge and was repulsed by a flank movement the Rebs masked the forces on the right and the right fell back then when the two boys was killed lias said they had to fall back to the support or be gobbled They fell back to the Support and brought the Rebs up a Standing Lias Said the Rebs held the ground that night and when they retreated they took everything they could Even the shoes off of the Dead Boys Our troops persued the fleeing rascals but Lias got permission to Stay So he got to See the boys before the ware buried I know that Lias feels like a lost Sheep being deprived of a Brother and a friend all of a Student that is Enough on this subject for it nearly brakes my heart to think of it The Devision that Lias is in is pronounced not fit for field duty So they are in Camp at Bridgeport Alabama Well Jane it is very cold to night and no prospects of it getting warmer for a while You must excuse my bad writing so no more at present yours as ever
Silas I. Shearer to E. J. Shearer

Well Jane this being the 18th I though I would writ a fiew lines more Well Jane the reason I do not write to you ofterner is this I am cooking for the Company and it keeps me busy and we have had no chance to Send Mail out untill here lately I will try and write oftener if I can. We was paid two months pay the other day and we Settled for our clothing and Uncle Sam Owed me two dollars and ninety five cents and he paid that in Cash so I got Twenty Eight Dollars and Ninety five cents and the boys paid me for cooking which amounted to Thirty Eight Dollars that is my wages for cooking I will not send any home at this time Tell Uncle Pery that John Mcgowen is a going to be first lieut.

Well Jane here is a picture I want you to take care of for me it is the photograph of our Galant Leader that led the charge at Black River Bridge I want to put in a nice frame Col Kinsman is his name Jane I want to know what kind of wether you had the night of the 18th I toled the boys Ide bet it was a snowing I must close for this time so no more at present youres as ever Silas I Shearer to Elizabeth J. Shearer You will find enclosed twenty five cts of new money and ten cents and Benty ten and Denna ten and the five you can give to the Babe it is all I have got to sent to the children.

Oald Indianolia Texas
January the 24th, 1864

Dear Companion This Evening affords me the pleasure once more of writing you a fiew lines and it will be an answer to a letter received from you the 17th inst. I am happy to say that this evening findes me well and harty and enjoying Soldiers life. I hope these lines may find all of you well and harty and enjoying pleasures of this world. Well Jenne we left Ft. Esperenza the 16th inst we got on a Boat and came to a place called Powerhorne. Our Regt camped in the Courthouse that night. It was something new to us to stay in a house and the next day we marched about three miles to where we now lay. It is about Eighteen miles from the Fort We are encamped at a very nice place We are on Matagorda Bay camped in a small town. We joined our oald Brigade again and the boys were all glad to see one another. Well we have a fiew Rebs within twelve or Eighth mile of here but they keep of pretty well They got five of our scouts the other day and we got one of ther'n in Exchange The way it happened our Scouts went out to see where the Rebs were and they out into there lines before they knew it Our party numbered forty while the Rebs were Sixty divided into three Squads. Twenty of the Rebs attacked our men and they out run our men and gobled five of them. The reason our men did not stand the Rebs afight was this. The Rebs out numbered them and they were afeared they would cut off there retreat and would gobble them which they most ashuredly would have done The scouts tokes it turn about in runing one an other one day our men will run them and the next day they will run our men The Citizens say here that Six Co of German Dutch has throwen down there arms and the Rebs keeps them under guard and further more a Citizen came from Brownsville and he sayes five Regt of Reble Calvary came in our lines and gave themselves up and have enlisted in our army. Whether this be true or not I cannot say If it is you probably will see it in a paper. Well Jane we had a nice oyster supper last night We have fresh Oysters here when ever we wante them and all it costs us is to go out and ketch them There is nothing any better in my estimation than a Dish of good Oyster and I think they goe very well to Eat them as I take them out of the Shell and Swallow them alive. It is fun for they go down so Slick Well Jenne we have preaching pretty nigh everynight in the Church. There was preaching twice today and also to night but I have not been up but once and then I could not get in. This after noons preaching was by a Dutch Citizen He preached in Duch for there are a great many Duch here. I was sorrow to hear that Granmother was Sick but hope she is well again. I would like to see her once more. I would like to se all of you again When I lay down of a night I have to think what a Happy we used to have but now we are fare from one another. I am out of Stamps and no chance of geting them here. I wisht you would send me some So no more at present your Husband S. I. Shearer to E. J. Shearer.

Oald Indianolia Texas
February the 7th 1864

Dear Jane This Evening affords me the pleasure of writing you a fiew lines informing you that I am well and harty as yet and Sincerely hope these fiew lines may find all of you Enjoying good health and prosperity. I received a very kind and welcom letter from you the date of it was the Seventeenth of January. It came to me the Sixth inst it was read with pleasure and would have been glad to read as much more. However I was glad that I had the pleasure of reading one that was written by you lovely hand It refreshes me I feel as though I had a friend that think of me although a great many mile apart we be but I think no less of thee and still go on for Liberty. I suppose from all accounts you have had a very disagreeable winter in iowa While we have had what you would call Summer I do not think it has froze more than a half a dozen nights and it is said to be the coldes winter for the last Six or Seven years but we have now such whether here as we have in Iowa in Corn planting It is very pleasant indeed The boys think it is very cool for the last twenty four hours. I have almost fell in love with Texas but I do not expect that I will love it well Enough to Mary. I expect when the War is ended my love will grow cold with Texas and I will forget the pleasures there of. You said the news as at Ft. Des Moines that we was ordered to California This is the first I ever seen or heard of. I would be glad if it was so for we would get in a health Country and A Country I have longed to see You need not be uneasy about us going there for we are in Texas and I think we will remain there A very good prospect at present I would as soon stay here as any place in the Southern Confederacy Well Jane my principals have changed since I last seen you When I was at home I was opposed to the medling of Slavery where it then Existed but since the Rebls got to such a pitch and it became us as a Military needsisity (I say us because the President is a doing for us the best he can) to abolish Slavery and I say Amen to it and I believe the Best thing that has been done Since the War broke out is the Emancipation Proclimation It has struck a death blow to Rebeldom so say the Rebs themselves and I want the thing to move a long untill the last blot of Slavery is wiped from this Union never more to return and it is Dying fast Louisiana is no more a Slave State Arcansas Mo Kenuck and Tennessee are all free and Slavery will not last long in Texas Now You may think I am foolish and you may call me a Abolishness as for that you can do as you please if you call abolishing Slavery Abolish I own the corner for I am in for puting the Rebs down and that to ther Sorrow So they may long remember it Now you may ask what will become of those Negroes that is left for the further. At the present the Negroesare all armed and made Soldiers made of they are good soldiers They learn to Drill quick active in there movements and have pride enough about them to make them hansom Soldiers I am going to try to get a Command in a Negro

Regt My officers say I can get a recomend I will try as soon as there is a Negro Regt araising her in Texas for Negro Regt will be kept to Garison Forts and that would just suit me I would go in such a place for five years Now you may hoot at this and say him go in to a Negro Reg Why he likes Negroes better than Me PaH!! What a Simpleton he is Well Jane as the General sayed to an oald lady in Tennessee when she complained to him about the Soldiers taken her Chickens he says well Madam we must and will put down this Rebellion If it takes the last Chicken in Tenn and that is the way with me We must put down this Rebellion if it takes me to be a Negro Officer.

Well Jane Fred Nichols has got back to the Regt and he sayed he seen you and had a long chat with you I was glad to hear of it for you could get some information about me He is not very stout yet. Well Jenna some of our Soldiers gets maried here They have enlisted in the Veterans and they get a furlough and by that means they get to take there wives home with them None in our Regt has married yet for our Regt are mostly married men Our Regt was out on guard review to day That indicates a March but whether it will be so this time I cannot tell Well Jane I wish as you did that I could be at home with you in my arms these cold winters nights for the boys say I am a very warm bed fellow I have wished to see you a great many times and kiss you sweet lips as I used to do We seen happy times once and Hope we will again I wish every night I had a sweet kiss from Jane. I never March never go to bed sit down but what I think of my Darling. I would love to see the children my respects to all Inquiren friends so no more at present Excuse my bad writing for I was in a hurry So no more at present yours loveing Husband Silas I. Shearer to Elizabeth J. Shearer

Indianolia Texas
February the 2nd, 1864

Dear Brother I received a fiew lines from you this Evening and I was glad to hear that you were well and going to school I think you are improving in writing very much I am harty and fat as a pig I am getting pretty nigh as large as Oald Potter I weight one hundred and seventy three lbs I hope this will find you well and harty. Well John twenty four of our Scouts went out after a Drove of Cattle today They went out six miles and was driveing in about two thousand head when sixty of the Rebs cavary attacted them. We lost between twelve and fifteen of our men Three was supposed to be killed and balance captured It is said one man out of our Regt was killed The Scouts cam in and Reinforced and went back and all they could find was some Dead Horses and two guns That is the way the Whelps do They watch around and when ever a fiew of our men go out they pounce upon them and do all the develment they can and then of again there is not enough of them here to stand a fight. The Rebs have no force this side of Matagordia to amount to anything and they are about Eight Hundred strong there Well John I will have to close you might excuse my bad writing for I am in a hurry so no more at present Silas I. Shearer to J. W. Shenkle

Oald Indianolia Texas
February the 22nd 1864

Dear Companion It is again I take an opportunity of writing you a fiew lines to let you know that I am well and hearty at present and hopeing these fiew lines will find all of you well and enjoying Pleasure I received a letter from you to day it was dated the 2nd inst I was glad to hear from you but was Sorrow to hear that the Babe was Sick but I am in hopes that it is well again I have not had a letter from you before this for nigh unto a month and I expected to see a large but I was some what fooled but at the same time I was pleased to heare from you If it had not been but two lines I could have read it with pleasure Although when I begin to read I like to read a large letter and I expect that is the way with you So I will not grumble It seems as though the letters you write to me dose not come as they should and the reason why I can not tell for you say that you write every week or two but myne are fiew and scatteren but I do not blame you for it I do not write only when I get a letter from you The reason is this When we are in Camp there is nothing new Occures It is one thing over and over so it would not interest you to read such letters. Well Jane we have had some tolerable cold wether again but it is pleasant at present We have a very comfortable place here I have taken a great fancy for Texas If it was a good a grain country as Iowa I would never live in Iowa The Climate here suites me to a Tewity The sun shines very warm but a breeze from the Bay makes it very pleasant unless a person gets in the Sun where the wind does not blow. How long we will stay here I can not tell Some say we will go to Mobeale but I think that is all a folly but a soldier has to go where ever they are ordered but I think if we leave here we will cross over on the Penenshula and go to Galveston Our Ordley is a going to Iowa to recruit and I wish we were paid of so as I could send my money by him We will soon have two months pay due us and then I will have very nigh a hundred dollars coming to me Well Jane I was to Church last night and I heard a good Sermond preached There were some ladies at church and it seemed a little like oald times for it is the first I have seen at Church since I left home but I could not enjoy myself as well as I could at home where I could see you I must close so no more at present yours as every Silas P. Shearer to Elizabeth J. Shearer

Indianolia Texas
March the 12th 1864

Dear Companion I take it as a pleasure to write a fiew lines in answer to a letter received from you March the 8th. It was written February 17th I was very glad to hear from you that you were all well again I am well and hearty at present and I hope these fiew lines may find all of you enjoying health and pleasure Well Jane what I can learn from your letters I get about one third of the letter you write to me I get a letter it comes very quick The letter I received had two Stamps on it They come in very good shape Well Jane you say you dont want me to reinlist You need not be uneasy about that yet for we have no chance as yet but probably will have before our term of Service is up I can not tell at present now what I would do I might enlist and I might not but there is no use in talking about that yet. I will try and keep out of that If I can You said that Mary Thompson has gone to Keokuk to se Bill and you imagine the pleasure that they have I cannot agree with you there For I could not see very much pleasure in being at a hospital or at such a place as that and here you come to See me I would rather see you at home if I see you at all I see more pleasure the way I am than to be at a hospital and you with me and you would think So two if you had the triall of it It is not because I dont want to See you There is no one on earth that I would rather Se than you I think a great deal of you and the Children I think of the pleasure we used to enjoy and the pleasures that is to come if we are permited to live I will know how to enjoy the home fireside. Well Jane we have had Preaching here for two or three weeks and they have made the Sinners Tremble and repent of there wicked way and brought them to a knowledge of the Gospel A great many of the Soldiers in this Division has repented of ther sins I rejoice to see it It would do my heart good if I could be one of them but my heart is so hardened that it was no impresion on me Although I attend the meeting. I have thought from what you have written that you are a praying women and if such be the case (for I hope it is) I want you to pray for me that the Lord will awaken me (as it were) from my slumber and to know a truth that the Lord is Good.

Camp Nigh Fort Esperanza Texas
March the 20th 1864 No 1'"""

Dearly beloved wife I take this day as a opportunity to write you a fiew lines to inform you that I am well and hearty at present and I Sincerely hope these fiew lines may find you all well and enjoying pleasures of this World I have written you a very short letter a fiew days ago and said I would write again soon There has been nothing of importance occured since I last wrote to you We marched from Indianola the 13th inst and encamped here on the 14th inst. There was a small accident happened as we was marching down here but not in our Regt We had two Bayous to cross We crossed thes Bayous on a Board constructed of several small boats probably you would call them Skiffs These small boats numbered three when the accident happened They were placed in the water lengthways with the Stream and Scantling fastened on them and plank for the flore and then the Board is drawn back and forth by a roap while the 69th Inidana was crossing the Boat sunk and twenty four whit Soldiers were drowned and some say Sixteen black Soldiers They got scared and drowned one another Some would swim up and down the Stream for a a hundred yards and would not go to shore So they would perish in the water But the boat was repared so there were not danger when we crossed Soldiers has to go threw a great many dangers and trilas in Battle or out of it They never know when they are Safe Well Jane I must tell you where we are and what we are a doing We are about four miles from Fort Esperanza a fortifying. We are building forts from Fort Esperanza a fortifying. We are building forts and breast works from a Small Bay Acrost the Island to the Gulf What is is done for I cannot tell unless it is a Fortifying against Foreign Powers This is one of the Prominet Points we have in Texas It keeps the Rebs from running Boats threw the pass so they cannot get there cotton and other traid out so they are dead in there Shell but I hardly think that France will interfeer with us. A hundred Thousand of our men could whip France in Mexico So quick that She would hardly know how it was done Probably you would like to know the reason It is this As quick as our men would get in to Mexico She would turn right a round and help us. Probably you think I do not know I have good reasons to believe such for it is all the French can do to hold the places that she has taken. Well Jane I want you to tell Uncle Pery that John See Charles Town and several others of our Co professes to be followers of the Savior of the World. See he no more like he used to be than day and night. Governor Stone wrote to our Colonel He said that two years of our time would be up in June and we could Enlist in the Veterans there after if we wished The Colonel wants the Regt to reinlist but how it will be is more than I can tell I do not think it will be necessary for us to reinlist Every thing showes a spedy termination of the War They may hold out untill after the election but that is all nonsence to them to do so with the calculation they have in there heads for I think oald Abe will be our next President If he runs I shall give him a Kiste Well Jenne the news came to Headquarters the other day that three States had came into the union by a large majority and we will be on our road home by May but you need not look for me untill you See me coming. We get all the fish we want to eat We have a Sane and we go to the Bay and ketch all the fish we want I am a going to number my letters so you can tell whether you get them all or not and I want you to do the same So no more at present yours as every Silas P. Shearer to Elizabeth J. Shearer

Camp Saluria Matagorda Island Texas
March the 24th 1864   No 2

Dear Companion It is again that I enjoy the pleasure of writing a fiew lines informing you that I am well and hearty at present and I hope these fiew lines will find all of you enjoying good health I received a letter from you dated February the 28th and it came to me the 22nd ist I was glad to heare from you and to learn that you were all well but was Sorrow to heare that the health of the Country was not good. The health of the Troops here are excelent We had one death in our Regt (CoB) the other day The first since we left Vicksburg and the nicest funeral I have seen since I have been in the Service He was buried in regular military form It looks nice when it is conducted in the rite manner Here tofore when the boys died so they were buried was sufficient. It appeared as though the Commandirs and Privates cared for no one but themselves I like to see respect paid to the boys in the Service as well as thought they were at home. I received a letter from Elias He was well at the time He wrote he was at Huntsville Alabama They took a Short tramp since the Battle of Lookout Mountain to reinforce a boddy of our ment which the Rebs attacted and drove them a ways and burnt up some of the quarters but our men ralied and put the Rebles to flight The Division he was in marched twenty three miles in eight houres and the principle part of that after night with Sixty rounds of Cartriges that I call very good marching but they did not have any thing to do with the Rebs Our men had whiped them out before they got ther So they marched back to Huntsville He says Huntsville was a place of between Seven and Nine Thousand inhabitants He says there is nice country around about the City He sayed he was at Church the other night and Uncle Sams boys and Secesh Ladies were the inmates of the House I will have to believe such Doctrin for I have had Experinece in Such caces but I like to Se women Secesh or not Although I am very Shy of them It has been So long Since I have seen them I hardly know what to make of them. Capt Dewey of Co G has two ladies withe him The talk is that he is married to one and the other one is hire (his wife Step Daughter) They are very nice looking women but I would hate to be in there place for they boys heare all kind of talk They have been out of Site of women so long a time that they never think of the conversation they should use when in the presence of the fair Sex and a great many of them do not care They have no respect for any one but at the same time we have to look over a great deal of there unbecoming language I do not wish you to understand that I am so very polite and throw all the blame on the other Soldiers I try to behave myself and use desent languarge when in the present of the fair Sex I will respect women of all kind whether black or whit unless they begin on me than they shall have the best turn in the Shop but it is very Seldom they pitch on to me for I am very civil You know that by Expereince that I never use any unbecoming language that will offend the ladies in any shape or manner I do not bother them very much and therefore they do not trouble me If they will let me alone I am sure they will not be troubled We have a fiew black women here in the Army I suppose there men are along and they stay with them and do washing for all the Soldiers they can That is enough on this Subject

will have to write a fiew lines more It will be filled with Miscelaneous items I have but very little time to write with the exceptions of the night We are working on fortifycations every day so it takes So it takes all of our idle time but the Colonel does not work us very hard We have got four forts very nigh completed We are a fortifying from the Gulf across the Island to a Bay Which is about three miles and four Forts are built in that distant and breastworks between them This Island is a going to be a very strong fortifyed place when these are finished There will be Six Forts with For Esperanza The Fortifycation we are at work on is about four miles from Fort Esperanza It is a mistry to me what they are a building such strong works for It certainly cant be for the Rebs There is none on the Island and only one place that they can forfit the bay" and one Regt can keep Five Thousand men at bay The ninety ninth Illinois are at that place and we do not have any pickets out to guard us while we sleep and the Rebs are very Scarce of Transports so they cannot do very much here This fortifications may be against Foren Powers but I do not think it necessary but it is well to prepare and if such a thing should happen we will be ready for them If any interfeeres it will be France but I think France is afeared to undertake such a job She will Rue it the longest day She is a governement for Rusha is a waiting for here to Strike a blow and she will. She will show her where her home is She has run her vessels out so as they cannot be blockaded A great many of her vessles are in our harbers a waiting for her to say what she will do. France has been trying to make a tready with Rushia but Rushia will not have anything to do with her. Rushia holds a grudge against here (France) Every since the Crimenian War and Frances knowes it Therefore I think she will not meddle any more than she has England has drawn of the trying to get in with us but I think she has sined away the day of grace She has detained several of the Rebels boats that they had built for them. I have a sneaken Idea in my head that if England could get France to decleare War with us and get her troops awsay from home that She (England) would light onto France and whail her herself She is that disposition here and France has been preparing for War for several years They do not like one another Well Jane I will have to taper off I seen Potatoes up from four to six inches high the tenth of this month And all other garden stuff was in like manners I like Texas first rate in such things as this but I think I will be satisfied with Iowas If I can get back to that good oald patriotic State I thought once I would like to go west but I have come to the conclusions that I will be satisfied at home once more Hank McGowen has got his commission for Captain I am in hopes he will make a very good Captain I expect some of the boys will get furloughs pretty soon There has several Blacks come to each

Company There are Sixty days furlough I do not want a furlough at present I would like to have a furlough next Summer if I could get it We had a considerable storme of wind and rain last night but we faired very well Our tents did not blow down I and Summers bunks together and Dave and Henry Perin and us four makes the little family of our tent We have very nice times I will send Denna a lottery bill if I had another one I would send one to Benta You must excuse bad writing for I work very hard threw the day and I am very nervous so no more at present I remains yours as every Silas P. Shearer to Elizabeth Shearer

Matagorda Island Texas
April the 4the 1864 No 2

Beloved wife I take the present Evening of writing you a fiew lines to inform you that I am well and hearty at present and I Sincerely hope these fiew lines will find all of you enjoying good health and pleasure This will serve as an answer to a letter just received from you It was dated March the 13th I was very glad to hear from you to learn that you were all well but was Sorrow to hear that you were so very much opposed to my going in a Colored Regt You need not be any alarmed about it The officers said I could get a recommend providing I could it would be uncertain of my geting suh a post for there is a great many recommends and no vacancies for them I do not think that I will try for such a place although I would suit me very well From the way you spoke in your letter it apears as thoug you care but little whether you get to See me or not You said you would not take a great deal for the hope of Seeing me when the three years are out and if I go in a Negro Regt you will have to give up all hopes of seeing me This is what you wrote for I have your letter by me but I did not think at the time I read it you ment what you wrote Probably you think if I like Negroes so well that I would not think of coming home to see you or forget that there was such a being as Jenna and the Two darling children but that is my first thoughts and then wandren thoughts comes on It appears to me that a person would do better and it would be (Better for the Government) to Stay in the Army untill the war closes Probably you can not see as I do I expect those women that are left at home sees hard and lonesome times Therefore you need not be uneasy about me Although the Veteran feever will rage high in this Regt when the time comes for them to go in Some Companys are readdy to go in as Veterans and pretty nigh ever man in those Companys I think two thirds of our Company will go in a Veterans Regt I would try a mans faith when the Companys goes in the Veterans to a man and what remaines behind that is higher than a private will be reduced to the ranks and be transfered to a Regt whether they are willing to go or not That is the way the thing has worked in some Regments Whether it will be so in ourn I can not tell and for the present do not care and I think the Veterans will get out very nigh as soon as the volunteers We are still on this Sandy Island yet when we came here we had to work on the fortifycations every day but we have got very nigh threw with that So nigh that they make details and the Regt do not go out to work but the fore part of the day is occupied with a Battallion or Brigade Drill and in the after part Skirmish drill which is a very good drill when the Soldiers know how to drill and it is conducted in the right way It is good excersise for me to go out and drill and hour or two and it is a great benefit to a persons health. General McClermane is in command of the Corps again The boys thinks as much of him as a child does of the Father General Fity Henry Warren from Iowa has command of the Devision at present The boys do not like him because he makes them put on to much Style but I think a great deal of him I like to see such Well Jane I have but very little money to send home at present I have loned it to Capt. John McGowen The reason I let him have it was because I had no chance of sending it unless by mail and I hate to reske it that way You need not think I am gambling my money is the reason I do not send any home I will save all I can and when I get a chance I will send it home where it can be taken care of I will send a fiew dollars which I have in my pocket So no more at Present Yours as every Silas P. Shearer to Elizabeth Shearer

New Orlean LA
May the 1th 1864

Dear Companion It is once more with pleasure that I embrace the present opportunity of writing a fiew lines to let you know where we are and how I am geting along I am well and hearty at present and enjoying Soldiers life the best I know how I hope these fiew lines may find all of you enjoying good health and pleasure Well Jane I received two letters from you the Evening before we moved at Matagorda Island to cros the gulf One was dated March the 20th and the other April the 6th I was glad to hear from you but was sorrow to hear that you and John was Sick but was glad to hear that you both were getting better and I am in hopes you are well ere this time and that your health will be good here after Give me good health before anything else I know how to appreciate health I have had good health for the past Eight Months and I enjoyed more pleasure in one month of health than I did the first year I was in the Service You write that the Spring in Iowa is very backward So it is in Texas but I am in hopes it will be so as the people can raise abundance of produce Well Jane we left Matagorda April the 26th on Board the Clinton for New Orleans We had a very nice time of it The Gulf was very smooth. We got to New Orleans the 28th We got off the vessel about dark and marched to a large building (which is called here the LaCotton press) and we are quartered in that building to the present and probably as long as we stay here I do not think we will stop long here but I long as we stay here I do not think we will stop long here but I can not tell where we will go to Some thinks we will go on up Red River Well Jane things are a great deal fowarden in this part of the Country than it is in Iowa When we was coming up the River while passing Fort Jackson one of the Soldiers while Standing on the Bank of the River with an arme full of large Onions (grown this year) he threw one on the Boat and as luck would have it it came to me So I devided with Henry Perin and it was as much as we boath wanted to Eat and when we got to New Orleans I seen all kind of Vegatables Turnips and Ceucumber which looked very good I seen corn knee high in New Orleans It all most made me home sick to See the trees in full blown Every thing looked delicate and Sweet It appeared as though we were going home Everything seemed to be cheering to the Soldier as they passed up the River the highest I was to timber since we left the Mississippi until we got back was fifteen or Twenty miles and it was a great treat to get to see timber Fort Jackson is a very strong place It is Fortifyed on Boath Sides of the River I presume there is nigh Two Hundred Guns in the two Forts It looks as though it would be imposible for Boats of any kind to pass it Nothing but Monitors could Esscape Well Jane I have been out in the City Twice since we have been here and I see a great many things that amuses me It is a great pass time to me to run over Town and see the beauties there of I have seen more ladies Since we have been here than I have seen here to fore Since I have been out some are very good looking Price Sommers and myself was down to St. Charles Theatre last night and it was Splend Dancing that can not be surpassed by any one Ladies and Gentlemen were boath on the Stage I got the worth of my money there if I never get it a gain A person can walk them selvs down and then they have walked over but one corner of the City Provo guards are Station all over Town and I have not been interrupted by any of them yet Generly when I go out in Town I mind my business and don't go to drinking and they will let me alone. I haven't been Tite since I have been in the Service although I take dram once and a while The Colonel let the Boys have a Spree when we got here and they had a merry time of it When ever we are away from any place like this or hard marching to do the Colonel gives the boys a day to Spree in he likes it him self and thinks the boys do Silas J. Shearer

Camp 23rd Iowa La
May the 11th 1864

Dear Father & Friend

We take the present opportunity (in the shade of a tree) of writing you a fiew lines to let you know that we are well and hearty at present with the exception of (David Perin) my wrist and hand which I got hurt on the Boat Well we went up Red River as far as Fort Duresse we could not get up any farther on the account of the Rebs Blockading the River they Sink enemy transport and gun boat that goes up unless it is iron clad We lay there three or four days and then came back to the Missippi we got up and down the River without any dammage from the enemy although we expected fire from them all the while we was gon We have been on board the Boat for Seven days and cannot tell when we will get off nor where that is to have our things off We go off and on when ever we land Well we are a going to send some money to you for you to divide David Perin Fifty ($50) Dollars for you to give to his wife and Silas I. Shearer Fifty Seven ($57) Dollars tend to this if you please and oblige

Youres as ever Silas I Shearer & David Perin

Camp 23rd Iowa
May the 12th 1864 No 4

Dear Wife I write you a fiew line finding an Opportunity (to let you know) where we are and how I am getting along I am in tolerable good health at present and hopeing these fiew lines may find all of you well and enjoying hapiness Well Jane we have had considerable of a Steamboat ride since I last wrote to you We got aboard a transport at New Orleans the 4th inst and went as far up the River as Fort Duesse and the Rebs having the River Blockaded we could not go any further We lay there for four day and then run down to the mouth of the Mississippi where we now lay We was in a very dangerous place while we were up there We was drowen up in line two nights while we were there The first night of our falling inline was caused by a fiew Cavalry with a dispatch from General Banks When they came to our Pickets they (pickets) fired on them and we fell in on double quick We soon fond out the Frakes No one was hurt The next evening a woman came to the Picket line and informed them of an intended attact by the Rebs about 10 Oclock We was ordered in line on the Bank of the River We lay in line that night with our arms by our Side The followin day we started down the Rivers Expected fire from the enemy all the while runing down and in fact when we run up ive expected it but did not received it We came pretty nigh geting our

78

Skelps taken the Second day that we was at Fort Duesse We went out one morning about half a mile after beef About the time we got the Beef ready to be taken to the Board The Colonel discovered the Rebs advancing on us from all direction except by the River The Colonel send orders for us to leave our Beef and come to the Boat as soon as possible Our Company was out without there arms The Rebs was trying to cut us off from the Boat which they would have done had not they been discovered The Colonel said that Twenty minutes longer would have done the 23rd We would have been under two fires from the Rebs The Capt and several others of the Boat that we went up Red River on are rank Secesh

Well Jennie Dave Perin and I have sent some money to New Orleans to be expressed to Marshalltown It will be Expresed in your Fathers name Dave sent Fifty ($50) Dollars for your Father to give to his wife and I send Fifty Seven ($57) Dollars for you Well Jane it seems as through the Rebs had the upper hand of us this Spring This Battle up Red River was foolishly lost by Banks mis management Cotton is what Banks is after and he will loose men to get it Fort Duesse was taken by our men every easy considering the position of the Fort It looks like it was imposible for men to Scale the walls but they went in with the Rebs opposeing them Prisioners that was taken at Pleasant Hill said that if we had whiped them there we would have had no more trouble that they were dishartened and did not expect to gain a Victory but by Banks mismanagement they gained the day and they have got very Saucy but for all this and the way the Rebs are cuting up on the Mississippi and other places I am not dishartened Our forces are mostly concentrated and the Rebs are doing this thinking to Scatter them but I think when we heare of General Grant moveing it make us rejoice and the Rebs to weep with Sorrow. Grant has got them in hot watter now They can not tell what he is a going to do I have a hard place to write so I will close so no more at present Your loveing husband Silas J. Shearer to Elizabeth J. Shearer

Well Father David Perin and I have sent some money to New Orleans to be Expressed in your name to Marshalltown the amount is One Hundred and Seven ($107) Dollars Fifty ($50) Dollars to Davids wife and Fifty Seven (57) to Jane When you get it hand Fifty Dollars to Martha Perin Youres as ever Silas J. Shearer Jane this Envelope will do for you to sent to some of your friends in the Army

Camp 23rd Iowa Morganzia Bend La
May the 24th 1864

Dear Companion I take this present opportunity of writing you a fiew lines to inform you that I am in tolerable good health at present and hope these fiew lines may find all of you well and in good Spirts We have seen prety hard times Since I last wrote to you We went up Oald River as far as the mouth of the Atchafalaya River and then up that River as far as Sims Port where Bankes forces was Retreating too To get acros the River Banks cros his troops in this wise he made a Bridge of Boats which they crosed with Safety it looked nice it will be out in Frank Liesles Pictorial Gen H. J. Smith had a severe fight with Rebs before we crost and he whaled them out After the troops were all crosed (which was the Evening of the 20th) we Started to march down the River We marched that night and the next day and the following night untill Eleven OClock We lay there untill 12 Oclock the next day and then marched three or four miles farther where we now lay It was very warm and dusty which we came down I do not know what will be next nor where we will go to I have heard that the 13th A.C. has been ordered on lite duty this Summer The 13th Corps very nigh gon up the two Devisions that was up Red River is very nigh all gon The 13th has seen harde times Since they have got under Oalde Banks It was a Corp that never was shiped before and Banks said he was a going to have it whiped once So as they could not brag of that So the boys say As we came down I seen corn that would very nigh cover a horse It was nice looking corn The fence was thrown down and the men rideing threw it in all direction Well Jane I received two letters from you and one from Elias and one from mother They came to me the 22nd ist yourn was dated April the 26th and May the 4th I was very well pleased to heare from you once again You said that Mary Shearer said for me not to go in the Veteran Service I think she is right I have came to the conclusion that I have had Veteran enough in mine if they had have kept me on the Island they might have got me but I think now I will serve my time and then quit for a while I have came to this conclusion if you will go with me to Washington Territory that I will not reinlist but come home a crop the Mountains I have read a great deal about that Teritory and I think it will suit me very well but I expect you will be against going there Well Jane I and Dave Perin expressed some money to father the amount was one Hundred and Seven ($107) dollars David sent Fifty ($50) Dolars and I sent Fifty Seven ($57) Dollars and I am agoing to send Ten Dollars in this letter for you Well Jane I would like to be at home to see you I would rather farm any time than to Soldier You must excuse bad writing for I have a very poor chance of doing it so no at present yours as every Silas J. Shearer to Elizabeth J. Shearer

Camp 23rd Iowa Morganzia Bend La
June the 2nd 1864

Beloved Wife I seat myself this after noon to pen a fiew lines which will serve as an answer to a letter received today from you It bear the date the 18th of May I was glad to hear from you once more and to learn that you were all well and that you had not forgoten me yet I am well and hearty at present and I sincerely hope these fiew lines may find all of you well and hearty Well Jane I havent very much to write at present but I thought I would write you a fiew lines to let you know where I am We moved two miles farther down the River since I last wrot to you We moved down on Sunday the 29th and in the evening the Regt was ordered to march at a minutes warning with two days Rations and Sixty rounds of Cartridge so you may know what it was for The Regt did not March until five Oclock the next morning when the Regt rolled out there destiny unknown to us but I heard since what they was after They marched somewheres in Twenty miles the first day but could not see many Rebs The Rebs would not stand a fight and they could not catch them So they maid a retrograde movement While they were marching back a band of guriles from the oposite side of a Bayough fired in to our men They killed a Captain and wounded 5 or 10 men of the 24th Iowa and wounded two or three of the 18th A.C. was all the dammage that was done Some of the boys that came in from the Regt Said that there was about two Hundred Rebs out there and that a Brigade of our Cavalry had run there horses down trying to ketch them but could not do it and the Rebs would not come close enough to fight them The troops marched within ten miles of here and Stoped and sent in for two days more rations What the movements are I cannot tell I was lucky once and did not have to go I was detailed for Comissary Guard the 30th of May and was not relieved untill the 2nd of June which is today I was very glad I did not have to go on one account and that was because my feet was sore from that march that we made from Sims Port to this place Well Jane it is raining today The first rain we have had since we left Texas and I wish I was at home a chating with you while it is raining I would like to see you all very much and to enjoy those pleasures once more and to kiss those Sweet lips which always was my delight to do that You know by experience as well as I do I never did nor never shall enjoy myself as well as I did when I was in your presence I write this from the bottom of my heart and if it makes you home sick or makes you feel like a lost sheep and do not like to hear such just write to me and let me know it and I most ashurdly will quit such writing for I dont want to disturb what satisfaction you do see I am willing to do any thing to make my love happy I must close for this time from your loving husband Silas J Shearer to Elizabeth J Shearer I send you another envelope that you can send to some of your friends in the Army You need not show this to everybody if you dont want to.

Morganzia Bend LA
June the 13th 1864 No 5

Dearly beloved Companion I Seat myself this day to inform you that I am well at present and I hope these fiew lines may find all of you enjoying good health and pleasure I received a letter from you to day baring date of May the 24th It was read with pleasure I was glad to hear from you and to learn that you was all well That is great Satisfaction to me it gives me more pleasure than any thing I can hear this letter will serve as an answer to youres Well Jane we are lying at Morganzia Bend listing for Orders to move the five Co of the23rd that is here has Orders to move today I suppose they are to join the other part of there Regt which is Somewhere below and I think we will follow soon Reports say that we are to go to Brashear for to guard that place and I have heard that we are to go to Batenrouge and Stay there all Summer I have heard that the 18th A.C. is to be relieved from Guard duty and be ready for field service and the 13th A.C. is to take there place and do garrison duty this summer because our A.C. is so badly used up but all this is not reliable Reports Our Regt returned from there Scout without any less or dam nage Our Cavalry is Scouting all the while to see what they can find now and then the gurriles takes some of our men in out of the wet Well Jane we had a general review last Saturday and it looked to me as though we had men enough here to whip the Western Confedracy combined if rightly managed While on review a heavy Shower of rain fell and wet us to the skin If the oald General got his Ass wet I dont care for the weting it has rained everyday since the first of June and how much longer it will rain I cannot tell Prospects is fare for more rain it does not rain stady probably from 3 to 6 showers through the day and then the Sun comes out and Shines hot enough to roast eggs It seemes to me to be the warmest weather I ever seen or experienced Some say it is not as warm this Summer as it was last but any now it is warmer than I like to See I like the cold country best although it is very disagreeable in the winter time but when Summer comes it makes it all up so we forget the disagreeableness of the Winter While the weather was cool last winter I was as fleshey asI could be but when the weather got warm I was not so fleshy but just as hearty as ever Except a week or tens days the time we Started for the Island I took a violent cold and was under the weather considerable and Marching down from Sims Port I was hardly able to march but under took the trip but we was marched so hard that I could not keep up all the way the last night we marched I could not keep up Downes he Staid with me and we marched on a ways and lay down for the night After we lay there an hour or two some Cavalrymen came along and told us we had better not stay there very long or we might be gobled in We rested a while and then went on inside of our Cavalry Pickets and then we lay down for the night after we got to our destination and I got a little rest I got better and am as healthy as ever This is the first time I had to fall behind since I got well last fall and am in hopes it will be the last I have nothing more to write at present You must excuse bad writing for I just came off Brig's Comissary Guard and I did not get to Sleep very much I was up untill 1 Oclock and then I awoke a Seargent up and let him run the Scheband untill day light So no more at Present your loveing husband Silas J. Shearer to Elizabeth J. Shearer

O yea I liked to forget I under Stand that you draw a County bounty If so I wish you would write and let me know You need not send me any more Stamps until further orders

June the 14th

Well Jenna as I did not get to send my letter out last night I will write a fiew more lines Seven Co of our Regt went out this morning at five Oclock to guard a Forage train Co E and K hapened to be the lucky Cos this time We did not have to go Co A is Provo Guards at General Lawler Head Quarters so they got out of the Tramp The Five Co of the 22nd Started yesterday to join the balance of there Regt where they will find it I cannot tell but it is down the River Somewhere The Third Division left yesterday for New Orleans I under stand the 24th and the 28th Iowa is in that Devision Gustus Cannon is in the 28th I have seen him several times also I have seen Smith and Milen Milen is ordly of Co K 28th Iowa Well Jenna it did not rain yesterday but threatened it very hard It is cloudy today Corn looks well here I have seen Corn here at present that is two feet higher that my head I have seen very good Corn in the South The greatest trouble with corn here is that it goes to Stalk and the Ears are very small but generaly tolerable sound the greater part of the corn that I have seen Since I have been South a kind of flint corn A person can raise any thing here in the South that they try unless it is wheat I havent seen any wheat here I think wheat will not do anything here The Mississippi River is runing down very fast since we have been here The papers say that it is geting very low above So as it will take Boats a long time to get up and down the River I under stand that there is to be Furlough given pretty soon I expect that Downes and Sommers will be the next to go I do not care any thing about going untill next Fall I dont want to go until the water is up so as I can go in a hurry I could have got a furlough last Spring from the Island if I had wanted it and the Capt told me that I could make it pay better by Staying with the Company at that time and I thought that Thirty days was two short a time for me It would take several weeks for me to get my visit out for I am a great fellow to stay at home I do not know whether I will get to come home this Summer or not I do not care whether I get to go or not Although I would like to see you but it cost considerable of money to go to Iowa and back It will cost $40 or 50 dollars to make the trip and I expect it will pay us better for me to stay and send my money home and have you take care of it It takes several month for to make that amount of money and it is well earned after it is made Two much so for me to throw away with out deriveing some beneft from it Several of the boys in our Co wants to go home very bad and I expect they will be the ones that will get to go first Pretty nigh half of our Co has been home on furlough and only two or three from our part of the Country Fred Nichols and Bill Thompson and Joe Misskimmins are the ones that went home and they did not to from the Regt Fred Nichols is very Sick at present in the Regmental Hospital Jane I want to know whether you got any thing for the rent of our ground and what kind of a crop was raised on the ground and whether you have got that mortgage paid off and every thing Square with Uncle Pery and whether he was willing to settle with you and let me know where he is and what he is a doing I want to know what the neighbours are a doing and how they are geting along I would like to know where Jake Crouch is and what he is doing and how he is geting along and what he thinks of the war at this time.

I under stand that E. P. Day is SubDirector of there Township I think that they were scarce of timber I suppose that Pote and Ably is not maried yet probably not likely to be for I expect young men are very scarce in that part of the Country at present So as it would be a dull show for a girl to get maried but a young man could get his pick of the flock. It is now guard mounting and I must close for this time youres as ever Silas P. Shearer to Elizabeth J. Shearer

Morganzia Bend LA
June the 13th 1864

Dear Brother

I must write you a fiew lines in answer to your kind letter I am glad to get a letter at any time and hear the good news that we are all well I am hearty at present and enjoying Soldiers life the best way I can and I hope these fiew lines may find you well and Enjoying the pleasures of this World I have Enjoyed Soldiers life very well for the past Eight or Ten Months and hope I can enjoy it for the next Fifteen months to come I under stand that the Coln Sayes he will start home by the first of July with the Regt as Veterans I have come to the conclusion that I am Veteran Enough and I think I will Stay out and serve say Fifteen Months and then go home and rest a while and then if I am needed I can reinlist if I feel disposed A great many of the boys think that the Veterans will get out as soon as we will that dont go in to it that is if General Grant is successful in takeing Richmond but I tell them no for this reason if Grant and Sheerman is successful in brakeing up the main Army of Rebels on the East of the Mississippi they will geurilly around for Two years at the least and of course the Troops will be kept in the field and the Veterans will have that to do Well John I am glad to hear that you are a geting a lot of horses on hand You and Your Father will soon have a horse team a peace and then you can make things get you will soon have horses enough and have some to sell every year if you had a lot of them to sell now you could make the money roll in When you write again I want to know whether you and you Pap is farming your place yourselves this year If you are you will raise a lot of grain if the weather is favorable so no more at present from your sincere Brother Silas J. Shearer to John Shenkle

Camp 23rd Iowa Morganzia Bend LA
June the 24th 1864 No 6

Dear Companion I seat myself today in as much pleasure as ever I did Since I left home to write a fiew lines in answer to a letter received from you It came to me yesterday and it was read with Satisfaction and pleasure as all letters are that are written by your hand I could read one every day with pleasure I expect it is the same way with you I was glad to heare that you were all well and enjoying good health but was Sorrow to hear of it being So Dry I fear it will be a great injury to the crops if you had some of the rain up there that we have had here it would have been a great help to the crops I am enjoying good health at present and enjoying Soldiers life as well as ever I did I sincerely hope these fiew lines may find all of you enjoying good health and pleasure I learn from your writing that you have a great deal of fals news concerning the Army I have had experence enough to know that it is policy for a person to not believe all such news unless it is confirmed You said that news was afloat about the Capture of the 23rd That was all a hoax We havent lost a man of the 23rd Since we have been up here When we started up Red River the Supposition was that we was a going to try to run a past the Batteries and that two Regt had been captured trying to run the Batteries Someone at the mouth of the River supposed we would be captured So we would if we had undertaken it probably The news went up the River aboard a Transport as far as Cairo then it was Telegraph to the Northern States as rumors of such things A great deal of such news is afloat and it creates excitement and uneasyness I never let such news trouble my mind I always wate for the Officials and then I can rely upon it We get some flying reports from Grant and Shearman but we just read it and talk over it until the officials come and then we Set it down as true but we get but very little counterfeit news from Grant and Shearman They are a doing the thing up so nicely that counterfiters have but little chance I expect you get a great deal more flying reports than we do our communications is by water and yours by lighting I see that Lincoln places all confidence in General Grants success over Lee at Richmond I think he is safe in doing so I think without a doubt he will succeed in taken Richmond The two great Generals of the United States has came together to try there Skill in the turning point of the rebelion and I think Grant has out Generald Lee I think he is the man that can do it He says all he wants is time to take us one Hundred Thousand men to take the place but according to there own (Rebels) report they are loosing as many men as we are I have know reason to dout it because they have made us many charges on our men as our men has on them and they are always repulsed with great Slaughter and So are our men when Repulsed Our men say when they are entrenced one man is good for three of them and I guess it is the same way on the other hand at Richmond anyhow but it dont seem to be so at any other place and there is Shearman Another hero of this Republic sucess and Renown seems to Crown his pathway and I hope it will remain so One thing has happened that I am well pleased with and this is the unanimous nomination of Lincoln for the Presidency I think he is the man that should fill that place for the next four years I do not believe a better man could be found in the United States at present I do not say that he is the Smartest man in the United States but he has been tried in that place and he just suites the Soldiers We have other men as good as Lincoln and probably would fill the place as well but they are untried and we donot wisht to try them at present and there is Andy Johnson One of the best men in the U.S. We find his name on the ticket for Vice Presidency he is a man that should be supported by all loyal men When his State Seceded he said no He would stay with the Union if oald Freemont runes on or excepts that platform of the Cleavland Convention or Excepts the nomination I think it showes what feeling he has for the Union and her Soldiers I have my opinion him or any man that Supports him I donot think they will accomplish anything I want you to write what you and the rest of the people think of the nomination of Lincoln and how they are agoing for the Presidency Whether any goes for the Copperhead or the Radicals as I term it your loving husband Silas P. Shearer to Elizabeth J. Shearer

Morganzia Bend LA
July the 1st 1864 No 7

Dear Companion I take the present opportunity of writing you a fiew lines in answer to a letter received from you I am well and hearty at present and hope these fiew lines may find all well and enjoy pleasure I received a letter from you dated June the 15th It cam to me yesterday It gave me great pleasure to hear that you was all well and was glad to hear that you was all well and was glad to hear that our money got threw Safe Dave Perin got a letter stating that she (Martha) received here money and it cost her $1.40 cts One dollar and forty Cts for the Express You wanted to know whether I though you used money foolishly I cannot tell as for that but I can say this much I did not think that you had as much money by you as you have I am satisfied that you use very little money The majority of the women use very nigh all the money that there men send to them I like to see women use what they need and not be extravagant for we Soldiers here in the Army earn our money by the hardest I was not raised to be extravagant and I do not like to see it I use some money but I generaly get things that will do me some good My tobacco costs me considerable Tobacco costs very nigh five cents a chew and that runs into a persons pocket tolerable fast I am going to send all the money home that I can and I want you to take care of it but I have seen enough of you to know that you will take care of money or anything else that is left in your charge I was some what surprised to hear that you was ready to crosee the Mountains with me I had an idea that you would rather I would reinlist than to go West

Well Jenne I expect when I get out of the Service that I will have an inclination of liveing in a civilized country I would almost as soon live in the South as to crop the mountains and live in the West A majority of the people that has emigrated West has gone to escape justice I would not live amonge them for considerable if I could help it A great many good citizens has gon there but not enough of them to cary the day If I should go any place I would rather go to Tennessee but I expect that I will be satisfied to Stop in Iowa You said that Denna was going to School I am glad to hear that he wants to go but I am a feard it will give him a disliken to it and to Study Sending him so young I want my Children to have good Education if he takes a delight in it and learns let him go If I should not get home I want you to give the Children good Education if you live Education is worth more to a man than a fortune in Gold Well Jane we are taken out of the 13th A.C. and assined to the 19th A.C. the 19th A.C is all Eastern men except our Division General Reynols command the Corps and Gen Lauler our Division General Lee our Brigade It is the General Lee that had command of the Cavalry forces up Red River from the appearence of things we will leave here soon but I have no idea where we will go We may not leave here for several weeks but we are to hold our Selves in readiness to move at any moment It has been very warm here for the past Six weeks and will remain so for several weeks More the health of the Regt is very good at present The boys are all well in our Company with the Exception of Williams Price and Fred Nichols They are bothe geting better Price did not go to the Hospital Fred Nichols is at the Hospital I have not heard from Mother Andrew or Elias for a long time It is something strange that I do not get from mother I received a letter from Elias about five or six weeks ago He said he had reinlisted and was going home in June and I did not write him a letter I cannot blame him for not writing I wrot a letter to Mother thinking it would get there about the time that Elias would get home I have not heard whether they went on or not or whether they are with Shearman a fighting there Corps is with Shearman the last I heard from them they were Provost guards in Huntsville Al I must bring my letter to a close as I have nothing of importance to write Exuse my awkwardness no more at present yours as ever Silas J. Shearer to Elizabeth J. Shearer

(Editor's Note: Throughout these letters, "Shearman" refers to William Tecumseh Sherman, commander of Union troops.)

Camp 23rd Iowa Morganzia LA
July the 7th 1864

Dear Wife I embrace the present opportunity of writing you a fiew lines in perusins those lines you will find that I am well and hearty and enjoying Soldiers life the easyest way I can I have soldiered long enough to not fret about anything if it dont go to Suit my fancy I sincerely hope these lines may find all of you well and hearty I received a letter from you today it bear the date June the 22nd It was received and read with pleasure for I seen nothing in it to discourage anybody but rather the other way I was glad to hear that Father was geting a long so well and pleased to hear that he is agoing to have a comfortable house to live in I expect he has to pay high prices for everything he gets or gets done toward the house I see by your letter that produce is very high that is hard on Soldiers that has to buy Everything that there familys use when they get such Small Wages I have heard some say that they cannot keep the familys with the money they get I expect it is so Some familys will use as much again as others but probably we can worry threw it if nothing hapens Well Jane you say you donot get letters very often from me I cannot tell the reason why I write very ten days or two weeks when we are in camp I answer every letter I get from you and that is tolerable regular Since we have been here there has been but very of intrust occured to my Observation Since I last wrote to you we moved our Camp last Sunday about a mile and a half down river We had a fine Shower while we was moving but it made us feel the better When we got dry we did not mind geting wet anymore We taken the place of some Eastern trops that went down the River they belonged to the 19th A.C I expect we will go soon it is reported that they are crosing Lake Pontchartrain in the direction of Mobiel Probably to attack that place If you had map of the Seat of War you could tell where we was and where we are a going to I think probably we will make an attact on Mobiel some time between now and winter Well Jane I was on Picket day before yesterday and came off yesterday morning It is very pleasant on Picket with the exception of one thing and that is Musquitos They are very troublesson here in the Timber Some of the boys say when they were on Picket they covered over so as the little animals could not get at them and that made them mad and they would pull the knapscack from under there heads I never had them to serve me that way yet The Boys that was on post with me got some Rostenears to Eat that was the 5th inst our Company and Four others Com was out guarding the wagons while geting brush Well, I must tell you how we Spent the 4th of July The 4th was greeted by a nation salute of 36 guns They ware fired at Sun up and at noon and Sun down (when I say guns I mean cannon) that was all that was done here in honor of our Independance Our Company was detailed to go as guards to the Brush to guard the wagons while geting brush I spent a part of the 4th in the brush a fighting musquitos and that is not a very pleasant take but have to put up with it Well Jane I will jut say if you spent any part of the 4th in the brush I hope that you seen more pleasure than I did and had not the musquitoes to bother you I would like to have been at home to spent the 4th with you It would be a great treat for me to get to see you again I suppose you have heard of the Soldiers wages being raised I think it is a good idea for one reason every thing is so high in price and Gold worth so much more than Greenback that a Soldiers family could hardly live Gold regulates the price of Produce and that brings it very high We have had some of the warmest weather here I ever seen it is warmer than I like you must excuse my bad writing I must close at present your loving husband Silas P. Shearer to Elizabeth J. Shearer

Camp 23rd Iowa St. Charles, Arkansas
July the 27th, 1864

Dear Companion I take this afternoon as a opportunity of writing a fiew lines to let you know where we are and how I am getting along I am in tolerable good health at present I have had a very bad cold since we have been here I hope these fiew lines may find you all well and hearty Well Jane we left Morganzia the 13th Our Brigade all moved at once four companys of our Regt went aboard the Universe and the other five companys aboard the Kate Dale Co. A did not go they being guards at Gen Lawlers headquarters and he is in command of the Division The Boats that brought our Brigade as far as Vicksburg ware as follows the polar Stare Univers Kate Dale and the Coln Colman When we got to Vicksburg our Regt all went aboard the White Cloud We run up to White River landing where the two companys of the 12th Iowa had the fight we lay there a day or two and then went on up White River We expected to be fired in to all the way up but was hapily disapointed we run up with out any trouble with the Exception of a Sand Bar which detained us one night and half a day the Troops had to get off of the Boats so as they could pass We run to St. Charles the morning of the 23rd Co H and B was throwen out as Skirmishers Our Regt advanced up the hill but we did not find the enemy we lay in line of Battle for an hour or so and then went in to camp we went to fortifying amediatly we worked day and night untill last night the Regt was devided in two Reliefes and they would take it by turns half a day and night each we are a geting fixed so as it would be harde to get us out of here our Company and two or three others of our Regt and detachments of other regts was out on a Scout yesterday but they did not find any Rebels I was luckey and happened to be on guard so I did not get to go Well Jane I expect you will think I have forgotten you but this is the first opportunity that I have had of writing Since we left Morganzia and I can not tell when this letter will go out the maile has gon out once since we have been here but I had no time to write I have not heard from you Since the Seventh of this month and can not tell when I will I have not heard from Mother but once Since we left Texas and I have not heard from Elias or Andrew for a long time I heard that the Regt that Andrew is in was in an Eighth days fight under Shearman and that they was badly used up I would like to know whether he got hurt or not I expect that Elias was in it to Shearman and Grant had done a great deal of hard fighting but they seem to be successful I understand that Johnson has Evacuated Atlanta well I am of the same opinion that Johnson is if could not hold the Mountains he can not hold Atlanta and the best thing for him is to get out and seek shelter some otherplace but I cannot tell where that will be Some thinkes that he will try and get to Virginia but that will not make it any better for him in the long run because they will have to have provisions and they have not got the provisions in Virginia to keep his and Lees Army if he goes there Shearman can go with him and he will be very apt to do it General H J Smith will be man enought to tend to the balance of the Rebls that is left I haint very particular how they worke it so as our men is on top Well Jane I would be well pleased to hear from you once more but I did not lay the blame on you I expect when I get a maile that I will get three or four at once I will write a letter to you when ever I can We are in 80 miles by water and 40 by land of DuValls Bluff and the cars runs from there to Little Rock General Lee that comands our Brigade is a nephew of the Reble Gen Lee He is a shrewed man and if the Rebles gets a head of him they will have to get up very Early I must Bring my letter to a close from you loving Husband Silas I Shearer to Elizabeth J. Shearer

Well Jane this is th 29th and as I did not get to send my letter yesterday I thought I would correct some mistakes that I made yesterday from the way you write Sunday comes one day soner here than it does where you live your letter was dated Sunday the 8th and where we was Sunday came on the 7th I came to look in my book I seen I had made a mistake in my writing yesterday I will now try and correct it We went aboard the White Cloud Saturday the 6th and the 7th a Sunday morning we started down the River and in the Evening we run a ground We went ashore but She did not get off that night we went aboard and lay there all night Monday morning the 8th we went ashore again. The Gunboat 28 drew the

Boat off We then went aboard again and run down to White River Station at the mouth of White River We lay there all night untill Tuesday in the afternoon when we Started down the River for Morganzia Now I want you to write to me and let me know whether you was sent mistaken in the day I have no doubt but you wrote the letter on Sunday but according to our almanac it was the 7th instead of the 8th. I put a letter in the Office for you while we lay at White River Station Joseph Thompson came to us while we lay there he has been harty every Since he has been back to the Regt Yesterday was the warmest day I every seen untill an hour or two before night It clouded up and after dark a little while a storm came up the wind blew and it rained very hard for a while I had to hold our tent to keep it from blowing over I got wet as a drowned Cat but I did not mind that As soon as the Storm was over we Spread our Blankets and lay down for the night but I did not get dry untill the Sun came out to day Sommers is my bunk mate he is a hard oald Cock We have ben bunking together every Since Dave Perin came to the Regt and that was at Indianola Texas Henry Perin and I had been bunking together I wish I had not give Henry up He is as good a bunk mate as I have had in the Army but Of all the bunkmates I have had there is none I like so well as the one I left behind I do not know how it is with other people Well Jane I am on Camp Guard today I was on Camp Guard once before and on fatique once Since we came back to Morganzia I am generaly very lucky about geting on Picket I havent been on Picket but very fiew times Since we left Texas Some of these days when I get time I will write some of my every day occurence off and send it to you Then you can see how often I come on duty Well Jane I would like to see all of you but I expect the chance is Slim untill my time is out Furloughs is not given to well men at present I would like to see Denna again and I would like to see Elen the one I have longed to see and see whether she has any Shearer blood in her or not If it wasent so much bother on a march to cary likeness I would like to have you and the children taken if they could be got natural The one I have got is not natural and a great many of the boys wants to see the Picture I will close for this time Yours as ever S. I. Shearer

Camp 23rd Iowa St. Charles Arkansas
July the 30th 1864

Dear beloved wife It is again I take the present opportunity of writing you a fiew lines which will be in answer to two letters just received from you I am well at present and Sincerly hope these fiew lines may find all of you well and hearty and enjoying pleasure I received two letters from you this morning I was well pleased to hear from you again and to learn that you ware all well Well Jane I was glad to hear that you ware at Newton the 4th of July I am in hopes that you enjoyed the 4th very much you seen to great many things that was pleasing to behold and it called to mind the cause of so many brave boys loosing there lives and a great many to be loss yet to this world I suppose you seen those glorious Stares and Stripes and the proud Eagle flying in the air and then to think that traitors are trying to trample it under feet and to make the Eagle bit the dust but the proud bird still keeps flying and begs them to come back and take Shelter under her wings and claim protection of the government but the traitors answer is know we will trample you underfoot and make you give us our independance Why it is enough to make the Stoutest heart quake to look on the Nations Banner and then to think that it must be cursed by such miserable traitors as inhabits our once peaceful but now distracted land I cannot see how copperheads can bear to look on the emblem of Freedom and claim protection and at the same time assisting the South in every way they can to encourage them to go on with there vile corruption I cannot see what they mean to Stay where they are and claim protection of the government and at the same time there heart and hand is with the South If I lived North and wanted to see the South Victorious I would go down South and take a gun I be a man or a mouse or a long tailed rat Well Jane you may think I am pretty hard So I am and cant help but we inducements has been given them that they could have came back and Saved thereselves and there country from ruin which it is a going to very fast I believe in treating them very harsh untill they come to some kind of terms and then round in Stoly on them We have had the news in the Memphis Bulatine that the Rebels had sent peace commishioners to Washington purposing termes of peace they proposed to come back in the union providing the United States would pay the debt of both parties and that they should keep what Negroes they have and the balance go free Now if they consider just the North the United States and that they Should pay the whole debt I am opposed to it If they would come back and beare there proporation of the debt I have nothing to say Well Jane I was surprised to hear that you had joined the good Templers It cam unawares to me but did not offend me in the least if you want to belong to it it is all rite if it does you know good probably it will do you know harm if it is conducted in the rite manner any one can belong to it that want to but it never did suit my fancy but that is know reason that you Shouldent belong I am in hopes that the lodge will prosper and that you will enjoy it very much Where ever a person can enjoy themselves there is where they should be   I never though very much of the lodge and therefore would have nothing to do with it it is more of a Speculating Sceine than any thing else Some man is filling his pocket off of the poorer class of people but if a person wants to belong to that lodge or any other one it is my will they should I suppose most of the folks in that corner belongs to the good templers It would not do for me to belong for we have been drawing our rations of Whisky while we had to be up of nights and work on the Forts We do not have to work of a night now We are prepared for the Rebs and we work at our leisure I got a letter from Brother

Andrew he was well They ware at Lost Mountion when he wrote I got a letter from Mother and one from Bob Heath and Ed Day they all came this morning They were all well with the exception of Bob he was not very stout but geting better I haven't heard from Elias for a long time with the Exception of a fiew words that Andrew wrote Andrew said he had been sick but was better and going to his Regt Andrew said when he wrote that they had been Skirmishing for Two weeks Well now it would be funny if Ed had Set Siege to Richmon and then would have to take it by a charge He would charge across the open field With Shining bayonets and glitering Steel But Still he would go with courage on untill he would come where none had gon and then he would stop and wounder why this Fort was kept so clean and dry and then he take it from the front I would not wounder if he would grunt So no more at present Your loving husband Silas I Shearer to Elizabeth J. Shearer

Tell Denna to be a good boy and learn as fast as he can and his Pap will bring him a new book when he comes home Tell Guy that I am all rite and my stomache all most strong Enough to Sleep with the wenches

Camp 23rd Iowa St Charles Arkansas
August the 6th 1864

Beloved Wife
I again have the pleasure of seating myself to pen you a fiew lines to inform you that I am well and hearty at present and I sincerely hope these fiew lines may find all of you well and hearty I received a letter from you today It was dated July the 13th it was received and read with pleasure as all letters are that I get from you I am allways ancious for the male Boat to come and then when the maill comes to the Capt Office and he begines to call over the names The boys will all huddle around him to hear him call there names and to get letters from there loved ones behind and if my name is called the thought Strikes me that that letter is from the one I so much loved and nine times out of ten if I get but one letter it is written by you and in a Short time I know what is in the letter I was sorrow to hear that the Chintz bugs has injured the wheat So much but I presume that there will be wheat enough raised to do the people and some to spare You write that every thing is so high that is almost discouraging to a person to be at home I cant see as you do and probably I do not look at it as a great many of the people do I under-stand that Wheat is Two Dollars per bushel Corn one dollar Oats 75 to 80 Cts and Say every thing else in proportion and then we will Say that factor is selling for one Dollar a yard Calico 75 Cts and mens ware is one dollar and 25 to two Dol-lars Now you see that a bushel of wheat will get two yards of factory and a

bushel of Corn will get a yard of Calico and so on in proportion and then we will go back three or four years and see what it was We will say that wheat was worth from forty to fifty Cts Corn ten to Eighteen Cts Oats ten to fifteen Cts Now we see that factory was from 18 to 22 Cts Calico 12 to 18 Cts and mens ware from 50 to $1.25 Cts a yard Now you see that a bushel of corn at that time would get a yard of Calico or a yard of the very porest kind of muslin and that time one bushel of wheat would buy two yards of factory and at two Dollars a bushel it will buy as good cloth for mens ware as it did as fifty and Sixty Cts a bushel from what I can learn every thing also is in proporation to the above mentions articles now I can not see what it is to discourage a person I cannot see but very little difference in the present and three or four years ago Only at the present Every thing is high in price and at that time only a fiew things was up Now if you will look at it rite and figure it carefully you will See that the is but very little difference Produce has went up so high that it makes up for the rise of other articles although I expect that a man that has a family and has to work out by the days work for to support it it may run him tolerable hard but I guess wages is as high again as they ware three or four years ago and I guess to sum it all up the difference amounts to but very little probably I cannot see Strait but it looks that way to a man up a tree Well Jenne I was surprised today I got a letter today the same time I got yourn It was a Strange hand writing to me I opened it to see who it was from and behold Jake Crouches name was signed to it it was the first letter I have got from him I had give up all hopes of geting a letter from him but when I least expected it one came Well Jane you can tell Uncle Pery that John See is dead He died the 4th of this month We have had four men die in the Regt Since we left Vicksburg two of them ware recruits the health of the Regt is tolerable good at present Well Jenna as I did not get to send my letter out I shall write you a fiew lines more this being the 8th We are now at White River landing We arrived here last night and will stay but a short time We left St. Charles the 7th we went aboard the White Cloud the Evening of the 6th from what I can learn we are going to Morganzia Bend Well Jane I received a letter from you yesterday it was dated July the 17th I was pleased to hear from you again You said that Uncle Wesley and Aunt Rachel was going down to Mothers this fall and that they wanted you to go along with them and you wanted my advice on it Well Jane I have this much to say that as far as I am conserned you can do as you please as I am not at home you can do as you please if you listen to anyone or want any advice ask your father and Mother they can tell you more about such things than I can for they are with you and I am not If you want to go I have know objections I am perfectly willing you should go I would be glad to hear of your a going but do as you please and you will please me You are at home and have controll of yourself and what ever you think best and what ever you can enjoy yourself that is what you should do. This is my answer to your question. Well Jane I will have to say a little concerning that question. I asked you about Lincolns nomination You did not answer my question at all I think from your writing that you donot like it yourself and for the balance I can guess at Well Jane I must close for this time we got off the Boat so as it could be cleaned and washed I will write you another letter as soon as I get to our journey end if nothing hapens from you loving husband Silas I. Shearer to Elizabeth J. Shearer

I will send the boys some presents as soon as I can take no offence at what I write.

Camp 23rd Iowa Morganzia LA
August the 14th 1864

Well Jane we are at Morganzia again but we are here awaiting orders A great many thinks that we are to go to Mobeal We left St. Charles the morning of the 7th and we arived here the 11th but did not go in Camp untill the 13th Well Jane I received two letters from you today The ware dated the 25th and 31 of July I could not understand what kind of a Doctor you have in Edenville I can understand that Egg Shell and Oil but the Ballence of the medicine I want you to write again I have not had the Diahrea since we was at Brashear last fall I suppose you told him how I was working and then he Supposed it was the Chronic Diahrea it is a wonder that as good a Doctor as he is Stays in Such a place as Edenville. Well Jane I am not agoing to write very much this time You must look over it for this time and excuse bad writing and Spelling for this reason I have the flu and it makes me feel very bad but I think I will soon get over it I hope this will find all of you well and hearty From you loving Husband Silas I Shearer to Elizabeth J. Shearer

Date uncertain - 2 years into the service
Keep this to yourself

Well Jane you said that Jacob Crouch lost his young mare that was a hard blow on him but probably he can get a long You Said you got those rings and leaves I sent you I am well pleased Pleased with your choice you think a heart is very nice. It is if a person can get a true one My heart has been with you alot it has been ever true to you Since I have been in the Army and I expect it to remain So Well Jane you said that Oald Jonny Crouch was going to leave that part of the Country and you thought it a fine thing. You said he had a man living with him that likes woomen You said he was a regular Whoremaster I would like to know how you

know all this whether you know it by Experence or whether you just guess at it or think it is so by what other people Say. Well Jane I have this much to say that if there is any War Widows and Girls that wants the Root I say for them to get it if they can and if they get knocked up it will not hurt me nor you if you let them and the Root alone A person that behaves themselves they will not Suffer such consequences My advise to you is this Say but little about such folks to the people where you live or any place in that Section of the County and behave yourself and not have anything to do with them Man Women or Girl and it will not hurt you or me Probably it goes hard with you to think that others gets it and you don't Well Jane I have this much to Say if I live to get home I want to see every thing all right and know stain on the family. Well Jane I do not know whether there is any more harm in Mrs. Barker showing the fruits of her labor than to keep it a Secret Well Jane I expect it is a good deal as you Say there has been so many deprived of that one thing they so much love that it is hard for them to get it but a woman should have some respect for there men and the men for there women. I have respect for my Beloved Wife and if I should live to get home than I can meet her with pleasure and not with grief When we go in these Townes we see a great deal of temptation to lead our minds from the loved ones at home My dear I would like to be at home and kiss those Sweet lips and embrace you as I once did I have not Enjoyed as much pleasure in the last two years as I did the last time I was with you Well Jane I wonder what Tilda Fattish thinks now of one man making twins I expect she has thought more than once about me telling Will that one man was not the Daddy of Twins When Ever you See a mark of a hand on a piece of paper keepe it to youself untill you find out what is in it if I write a peace I dont want everbody to see I will make a mans hand on it you will know then what to do I will close this
you loving husband Silas I. Shearer to Elizabeth J. Shearer

Camp Near Tilton Georgia
August 22, 1864

Dear Sister I will for the first time in my life try and interest you with a few lines. Informing you that I am well and trust this may find you well. I have often wished to hear from you which I hope will soon bring a Speedy answer. This has been quite an excitement here but is now all quiet and everything working well. Wheeler the Rebel General was confident of sucess by making a raid wich he failed in most all his attempts. They tore up some Railroad took Dalton but was soon driven out again. They also capured two Co's belonging to our Regt. Prisnors but have parolled them and they are now back again. These parolls is not recognized by our Government so they will take arms again. This scare was yesterday

and today a week ago they have gone in the direction of Middle Tenn. They were whiped at Dalton and then they went to Cleveland Tenn where they were again whiped. They have done but little damage yet considering there force. They may yet do us some damage I think our Gens. will have there eyes open watching them and be prepared for them. I have not heard from Silas for some time. I don't know how he is nor at what place he is at. I never have received a letter from home for sometime. I have been writing to Uncle Wesley's Family but have not received a letter for sometime. I also sent Polina my photograph which I suppose you have seen. We have fine times here living on the fruit of the Country. Peaches are now ripe and are splendid. Apples are mostly all gone I see no prospect of going on Veteran furlou. I think we will go home when Atlanta Falls in our hands which may be sometime yet. news from the front are most all encouraging. We are most always sucessful in all our movements. Our Div has been quite lucky this campaign. Our Div has always been together ever since we come out and was organized into a Div. We always have been in the front till this Spring Campaign. I would not be surprised if there would be some trouble in some of the States about the time the Fall election comes off but I hope all may pass off smoothly. If our Fall elections goes in the right channel I think then the War will not last many years and if such a man as Vallandinghava should be elected for President I dont know what would become of us and our Government which we are Sustaining. I believe we would go to ruin at once although I am confident that Abe will be our next President. I will close on this subject not knowing what your sentiments are. I will close on present hoping soon to hear from you.
Yours with respect Elias Shearer to Elizabeth Jane Shearer
Direct Co # 17th Regt Iowa Inftry Via Nashville, Tenn

Camp 23rd Iowa Morganzia LA
August the 28th 1864

Beloved Companion Youres of the 8th Ist arrived yesterday the 27th It was gladly received and read with pleasure I was sorrow to hear that you and mother had been Sick but was glad to hear that you was well again and that mother was better I love to hear of health in the family I am well and hearty at present and I Sincerly hope these fiew lines may find you all enjoying good health Well Jane I am sorrow to hear that you are so lonesom and that you have such a poor chance of going to meeting I wish I was at home so as I could go with you and help take care of the children but probably it will be some time yet before I can be at home but if I live twelve month longer I will think considerable of being at home with those I so much loved You said in your letter of the 8th that you wandered where

97

I was and what I was a doing Well I can tell you Exactly where we ware and what we was a doing We left St. Charles on Saturday morning and run down White River and in the Evening we run a ground and could not get off We lay there all night and Sunday morning (th 8th) we got off of the Boat The gun Boat 28 pulled the Boat off We went aboard again and run to the Miss River and landed at White River Station We went a shore so as they could wash the Boat We lay there untill sometime in the Afternoon when we went aboard and run down the Miss River I can tell what I do every day I Set it down so as I can see for myself I enjoyed myself the best I could that day but there is but very little pleasure for a Soldier on board a transport Joseph Thompson came to us while we ware at White River landing He has been harty ever Since he came to the Regt We buried one of our boys (Co K) Since we got back to Morganzia Downes is Sick at present but is geting beter The balance of the Boys are well You said you heard that we was at Washington we are not there yet when we came down the River we thought that was where we was a going the 22nd 24th and the 28th Iowa has gone there It dont make very much difference to me any more where we go The Supposition is now that we will be kept on the River I do not like this place It is very hot here at present and I think it is a Sickly place The nicest place I have Seen Since we left Texas was St. Charles it is very high and a nice breeze all the time and we could get Apels and peaches and Rosten Ears and Beef here we do not get any of such things we have to live on such stuff as Uncle Sam gives us and the Boys gets tired of that Probably we will get Potatoes soon Well Jane it has been nigh four months Since we have been paid any money The first of September will be four months I heard that we was to be paid soon after we was mustered for pay and that will be next Wednesday Jane I want you to send me one dollars worth of postage Stamps I have had no chance of geting any I save money to get them So you will not be out any money What money I send home I dont want to make use of for I generaly keep enough for such as that I bought Stamps when I was in New Orleans but I have used them I cannot write many more letters untill I get Stamps You said you wanted me to get my likeness taken standing when we are paid I will have it taken if there is a Shop here It will cost me two dollars to have one taken Standing but I donot care for the price if it will be any pleasure to you I will do anything that I can to please you I received a letter from Robert yesterday He said if he was in my place he would want to go home and see those brite eyed children He said he had the children likeness he said they ware smart looking children I would love to see them I would like to see Denna again I would like to see Elen to see whether the was any Shearer blood in her or not She is a child I have longed to see but I do not expect to see her untill my time is out if I live untill my time is out it will not take me long to go home from where I am discharged I will not wast many minutes in going A great many in our Regt thinks we will not have to serve our time out I would be happy if that was the case but I cannot see it at present Although Hoods Army says they will hold Atlanta to the last Gen Hood says if they cant hold Atlanta it is no use of them trying to fight any longer for they cannot do any thing that is sound advice in him if they can not hold that place they had better give it up Deserters have came into Shearmans Army Some say that Hoods Army is discouraged Some say they want peace and some of them say they are a going to fight it out there that is what I think I think that Army will not do very much more fighting after they leave Atlanta If they dont leave soon Shearman will take them with him when he goes The Rebels say that Mobeal will fall in to our hands They think it is imposible for them to hold it Well Jane Fred Nichols has gon home on a furlough I sent with him three finger rings one heart and two leaves to you They are maid out of a Claim Shell it is some of my own make if you get them I want you to take your choice of them and then devid the balance among the other children. I do not mean just our own write to me whether you get them or not

From you loveing husband Silas I. Shearer to Elizabeth J. Shearer

Traitor
Part of Earlier letter

Well Jane as I did not close my letter last night I will write a fiew more lines. It is warm and cloudy this morning it has the appeerence of rain. We just came in from Company Drill and I am nervous so you must excuse bad writing. Well Jane I received one of these oald letters a fiew days ago, I was glad to read the letter although I had later news from hom than it was. I probably never will get the other letters the latest letter I received from you arived the fifth of the month Well Jane, there is to be a man Shot to death here this afternoon at Two Oclock. I understand that the Troops is all to be marched out to see him shot. He deserted our Army at Shilo and went to the Reble Army and gave them all the information he could concerning our Army. I heard that he maried a Reble Majors daughter and he gave him Twenty Five Thousand Dollars. Some say he was captured bushwhacking and others say he enlisted as a Teamster for our Army and he was caught Smugling Amunition to the Rebles, I will stop writing untill after this afair goes off then I will finish the letter if nothing happens, Well Jane we have just got back from seeing that man Shot there was about Five Thousand Troops present, Two Batteries, and some Cavalry. I never want to see an other man Shot although he deserved it. The Orders said that he received five different Bounties from the United States he belonged to the 32nd Ohio. Tomorrow morning at nine Oclock we will have a general Inspection I must close so no more at present yours as ever S I Shearer to E. J Shearer Excuse bad writing

Camp 23rd Iowa Morganzia Bend LA
September the 4th 1864

Beloved Wife I this afternoon enjoy the pleasure of writing a fiew lines to inform you that I am well and hearty at present and I sincerely hope these fiew lines may find all of you Enjoying good health I received three letters today one from you one from Mother and one from Elias youres bare date of August the 23rd I was glad to hear from you again the letter I received from you before this was dated August the 8th I began to feel lost it seemed to be a month since I got a letter from you Mail after Mail came but no letter came for me untill today I received one from the one I long to see I was very much pleased to hear from you to hear that you ware all well again Well Jane from what you write there is considerable of emigration to Iowa or will be this fall I am glad to heare of Emigration to that State it will make times a great deal better Well I do not know but if I had the chance I would Emigrate to Iowa and settle down and reamain there I like that Country better than I do this for farming Well Jane I received a letter from Mother today They ware all well when she wrote She said that they had not heard from Andrew Since the fight they had She says he is taken prisinor or killed and what she writes he is as likely to be killed as a prisioner Uncle <u>Fetty</u> seen one of the boys of the Regt he was there but not in the fight he said they faught like Demons and the last they was seen of they ware cuting right and left they Said they would not Surrender but they ware surrounded by a large force but the most of them ware killed and taken prisinors The 8th Cavalry has Equaled the 2nd Cavalry while they lasted I have been uneasy about the boys all Summer but finly heard from them and untill I hear from Andrew I will be uneasyer than ever if he is a prisinor in that part of the Confedracy he will be treated very bad They treat prisinors a great deal worse in that part than they do on the West side of the River where we are I am a feared he is killed or wounded and fell in there hands it seems as though the Regt that the boys has gon in are Regt that could be depended on and they are generaly put in the hotest of the fights Well Jane I received a letter from Elias today he was well when he wrote you bet I was glad when I found it was from him for I had not heard from him since April last He said they ware at Tilton on the R. R. running from Chatanooga to Atlanta They are guarding the Road they had not been in any fight when he wrote He said they ware having fine times they had all the green fruit they wanted They had all the girls and women they wanted he said they had (Well Jane I will send you this letter and you can read for yourself) We was Mustered last Wednesday for pay but have not seen the paymaster yet We may be payed soon and we may not Well Jane Bill Thompson came to the Regt the 1st Inst pretty nigh the first thing he said to me was well Sile I seen you wife and had a long chat with her I was glad he went up to see you he could give me a great deal of satisfaction He could tell me how you are geting along I asked him a great many questions Some he could answer and some he could not He talked very flatering of the Children especialy of Elen he said she was the pretiest child he ever seen It was very flatering talk to me I would love to see that child I could tell whether it is as pretty as it is represented to be I would love to see Denna and see whether he is as Spunky as he used to be Well Jane we had Orders the Second of this month to go aboard a Boat yesterday morning at Six Oclock but the Orders ware Countermanded The 7th Reg 37th Ill and 42nd Ohio of our Brigade and the 21st Iowa out of another Brigade Embarked in the afternoon of the same day I understand they are Ordered to Report at the Mouth of the White River We may leave here soon and we may stay Sometime yet our Regt and the 35th Wis is the only Regt of our Brigade that is here Well Jane I must close for this time So no more at present from you Husband Silas I Shearer to Elizabeth J. Shearer

Matagorda Island Texas
"The Kingdom's Coming"

O Darkies have you seen the Massa
With the Moustach on his face
Go down the road sometime this morning
Like he's goin to leave the place
He sees the Smoke way up the River
Where the Lincom gunboats lay
He take his hat and left very sudnt
I spect he's rund away

Chorous Oald Massa run ha ha
and the Darkies Stay Ho Ho
I must be now the Kingdom's coming
and the year of Jubelo

He's Six foot one way two foot the other
And he weighs three hundred pounds
His coat so big he couldent pay the tailor
And it wouldent reach half way round
He drills so much they call him Captain
And he gets so dreadful tand
I spect he'll try to fool dem yankees
and think he controband

Chorous Oald Massa

Ode Darkies gets so very lonesome
In de log hous on de lawn
Day'll take dare things to Massas parler
For to keep em while he's gon
Dare is wine and cider in do cellar
And de Darkies day have some
For I Spect we'ss all be confiscated
When the ol Lincon Soldiers come

Chorous Oald Massa

De Oberseerer makes up trouble
and he riches us round a spell
We'll lock him up in the Smokehouse Cellar
Wid do key thrown in de well
De Whip is lost de hand cuffs broken
and Oald Massa gets his pay
He big enough and olad enough and ought
to know better than to went and run away

Camp 23rd Iowa Morganzia Bend La Sept the 13th 1864

Beloved Wife Youres of the 7th Inst arrived yesterday the 12th It was gladly received and persued with pleasure I found it contained newes that I always like to hear and that is the health of the family being good at present and I sincerely hope these fiew lines may find all of you well and Enjoying pleasure I received a letter from you Since I last wrote to you but it was an oald one so I did not answer it So this letter will be an answer to boath of them Well Jane we are at Morganzia yet and no Sines of leaveing Soon but we may be ordered on a Boat and leave before Morning The 20th Iowa is in our Brigade now and I understand that the 19th and 34th Iowa is to be in our Brigade We have been with Iowa Troops before and they would do to tie too they would Stand Nobly to the works as fars fighting and Marching We have Escaped very well this year but whether we will fair as well the balance of our time I cannot tell Some thinks there will be an Expedition for Shrievesport (on Red River) this fall but I cannot get in my head that way although I may be mistaken I would not mind taken a tramp threw the Country after it gets Cool The weather is geting Cooler here it is warm threw the day and Cool of a night Well Jane I seen in the papers that two Commishion officers and Ten men was all that Escaped of the 8th Iowa Cavalry and I guess it is certain that Brother Andrew is amonge the missing I guess Gen Hood has got out of Atlanta by hard fighting and Sherman has give him a complete thrashing Since Sherman is the man that can whip him but he did not want to run him out of Atlanta but Hood could not bear so much flank movements he got Scared and thought he would leave and it was hard work for him to make The rebel Johnson would have whiped Sherman a great deal easer and quicker (he would have kept retreating) and Sherman would have followed him and he would have got a great ways from his base of Supplies and it would require such a large Army to fight him but the people in the South as good deal like the people of the north if there (the South) Gen retreats before our men to save his men they get dissatisfied and say he is no account That is the way with the North if our general lays Siege to a Reble town and they can not take it in a week or two they get dissatisfied and growl about it as though they knew more that the Gen where they should keep still and trust to him I will close You loving Husband Silias I. Shearer to Elizabeth J. Shearer

Camp 23rd Iowa Morganzia Bend La
Sept the 18th/64

Dear Wife

I seat myself this Sabbath Morning to answer your letter of the 8th inst it arived the 16th Inst I was glad to hear that you was all well I am well and hearty at present and I hope these fiew lines may find you and the connection all well Well Jane I hardly know what to write We have been lying Still for Sometime and I have nothing of interest or anything that would likely to interest you and therefore I will have to write Such as comes to my mind first The letter will be of little information foolish and know account We had general inspection yesterday and Company Inspection this Morning and I have had but little time of collection my thoughts to write a letter that would be likely to interest you. I said we had been here for Sometime we may leave here within Six hours but we would not be likely to be gon more than three or four days probably there's force Enough gon to accomplish the work Our men has been Skirmishing with the Rebs and I understand that they (Rebs) have retreated acrossed the Atchafalaya (the pronounciation of the word is Achafalia) and they are Skirmishing acrost the above named Stream I under stand that a force of our men is Sent around in the rear of them to goble them Whether they will be Siccessful or not I cannot tell I heard that they (rebs) had taken Seventy five of our men and our men had taken Eighty of the Rebles. I cannot tell whether it is so or not but one thing I do know

I heard Cannonadeing yesterday morning between two and three Oclock I was on guard and was up the afterpart of the night and I heard about a dozen shots fired It sounded natural to me and yesterday while on inspection a gun boat shelled the woods All of this sounds as natural to us as it does to hear them call for dinner We may not be called to assist in this Scout the Reble force is estimated at 1800 Our boys killed and wounded is very light Well Jane we have an oald Regular in Command of our Brigade and he makes us drill twice a day Company drill in the Morning and Battallion drill in the Evening and Dress aparael at night but that is good for our health but some of the boys growls Some would growl if the General would feed them on Sweet Cakes and pies Well Jane I have been to dinner and I will go on with my foolishness Well I said some boys would not be satisfied feed on Sweet Cakes and pies but I am satisfied with hard tack and worms in them half an inch long and bugs that would weigh a pound Since I have went so far I will explane myself We have had the poorest grub here at Morganzia that we ever drew Our meet and coffee is as good here as anyplace we have been but our Crackers is pretty nigh all wormy We draw some flour and get it baked beans rice and sugar is the same here as any place else It is not the Governement falt that we get Such grub it is the Quartermasters falt Our General Says we shall draw flour while we stay here potatoes and Onions we cannot get at present They are very scarce yet Potatoes are worth $7.20 Cts per bushel here but I am hearty now and I can eat any thing that anybody else can but when I am not well it goes hard to Eat such grub The greatest trouble with us now is Tobacco We have no place to buy of and haven't been paid for Sometime So we have to do the best we can I think we will be paid soon Well Jane Bill Thompson is proud of his girl when the letter came to inform him that he was father He could not rest untill I read the letter Well I dont blame him for that The boys try to plague him but can not make anything off of him This is the pleasantest day I have seen this side of Texas this year we have tolerable cool nights but generally warm days it is foggy of a Morning and that you know is aguish weather I wrote sometime ago for you to send me a dollars worth of Stamps and if you did not send the Stamps send them on recit of this and you will oblige me I must close by saying our Regt will go for Lincoln by a large majority Well Jenna to morrow will be two years since we was Sworn into the United States Service one year from today if I live I will think considerable of seeing Jenna and the two Children if they live
your Husband Silas I. Shearer to Elizabeth J. Shearer

Camp 23rd Iowa Morganzia La
October the 11th 1864

Beloved Wife I Seat myself to write you a fiew lines in answer to two letters received yesterday They bare date September the 18th and 25th I was pleased to hear from you again I heard from you the 16th of Sept and we had to go out in the Country we was gone ten days Therefore I did not get a letter from you untill yesterday it was read with pleasure I was glad to hear that you and the family ware all well and hearty Well Jane I expect before this arives you will think I have forgot you but not so I will tell you the reason I did not write before this I wrote to you the 17th of Sept. in answer to a letter I received the 16th I answered the letter and Expected another one in a week or two but did not get any and being out of Stamps I did not write and on the 30th of Sept we got Orders to March We marched on the first of Oct We marched out on the Atchafalaza for Some purpose I know not what for We did not accomplish any thing that I could see It is about 35 miles where we was and to day I thought I would answer your letters We had a good time while we was gon although it was a Skitish place for Pickets One man in Co H of our Regt was Killed he was shot while on post he was Shot from a house After that hapened our Men soon layed the houses to the ground by applying the torch We got to Sims Port the Second Day our advance was Texican Cavalry They had a little Skirmish acrost the River The Cavalry lost one horse that was all the damage done that evening Although the conclusion that we should not have waters to cook with The Rebles ware consealed in the brush on the oposite side of the river (the river very narrow) When the cooks would go down after Water the Rebs would fire at them from the time they would go over the bank untill they would get back but that soon became a two handed game but they did not care for that untill they got a fiew Shells from the Battery Them was rather larger Balls than they liked to fool with haveing none of the kind to throw at us. In the night Co's G.H.F and A of our Regt and Some Co's of the 20th Iowa and 35th Wis ware set acros the River in yawis that we had taken along for that purpose There was but fiew Shots fired at them while crossing The Balance of the three Regts and the greater part of the Cavalry was left on this Side This all hapened about two miles above Simes Port We got up the next morning very early to March the two miles the 20th Iowa was sent down with the Battery while those Co's would gain a position on the oposite side of the River The Battery shelled the Woods but could not get an answer then the balance of the troops was ordered down while we was marching along One shot was fired from the oposite Bank The Shot was aimed at the Commander of the Regt but it done know Damage After we got down in front of Sims Port we went in Camp making our selves as Comfortable as posible Our Commander had some Cavalry Set acros to Scout The Cavalry and these Co's that was acros went farther out to see whether they

could find a force All they could find was a fiew Scouts after they came in and reported no force very nigh us the troops ware sent to the Regt with the Exception of the four Co's of our Regt They ware kept on the oposite side untill we got ready to leave it was a very Skitish place the Pickets was fired on frequently and only one man hurt and he was Co H man Pretty nigh every night the Rebls would shoot acros at the camp The 35th would have tolerable large fires and then huddle around it to keep warm by so doing the Rebs could see them very plane and then they would let into them The balls would Sing over our heads Co B and K lay in range of the balls that came from the Jonnies but there night Shooting done no damage to the troops When our men would open with the Artilery the Rebs would Soon play quit The last night we was there the weather was tolerable cool we had a fire and was Seting around it a keeping warm and Spining Yarns The 35th was in like manner and the Cavalary on the left of the 35th had there fires we was on the right of the 35th The most of the Boys of our Company had got tired of yaking and layed down I hadent layed down but a fiew minutes when the Rebs Commenced throwing at us there Shots ware Directed to the Cavalry and the 35th Our Co being in range with the 35th caused the balls to whistle over our heads The Cavalry returned the fire News came to our Regt that the Rebls had crost the River and was coming in We was ordered in line to meet them but it prooved to be from the other side of the River A fiew Shot from the Battery Silenced them we then went to bed and Slept unmolested that night and started back the next morning before daylight. A flag of truce came to our lines Capt Cross of our Regt talked to the Capt of the flag of truce The Rebl Capt Said that they ware whiped he said that if they would Surrender that we would allways be throwing it up to them that they ware traitors they donot like to give up to the North but I think they will have it to do Well I will drop this Subject Well Jane I received Seven Stamps in one letter and Thirty in another one I also received you likeness Well Jane I must say that I never Seen you look so Fleshy I would hardly have knowen the picture if you hadent writen who it was it is as good picture as I ever seen but some thinks your other picture is the best looking the last one is the best picture but it dont look as natural to you as your other picture does I dont remember of seeing you so Fleshy as you was when that picture was taken You must have Someone that takes better care of you than when I was at home but how ever I am glad to see you hearty from your loving husband
Silas I Shearer

Camp 23rd Iowa Duvalls Bluff Ark
October the 20h 1864

Dear Wife I take the present opportunity of writing a fiew to let you know where we are When I last wrote to you I had to stop writing before I got my letter finished I said in the letter that we had Orders to move imediately but I did not know where We went aboard the transport Nebraska and ordered to report at the mouth of White River We went aboard the Boat the night of the 11th and the morning of the 12th We Started up the River we arrived at the mouth of the White River on the 16th There we got off of the Boat and the next morning we went aboard the Transport Shenanga bound for Durvalls Bluff we arived at Duvalls Bluff in the after noon of the 18th we went in camp as though we ware agoing to stay awhile notwithstanding theirs a great deal of talk of our going to Fort Smith I hardly think we will go there I would like to go there very well I would get to See the Country that I have longed to See Well Jane there is considerable of improvements a going on in the south A Woolen Factory is building in Vicksburg and also a new Cotton Ginn the Ginn is in operation Considerable of improvements are going on here at the Bluffs A large Depot is building it is quite a business place mechanics get Four Dollars a Day Cash for work and also a Circus is to be here tomorrow and next day but we are poor boys We have know money we cannot go but when we get our money we will have a lot of it Well we was lucky in geting up White River The was not a shot fired at us we have been very lucky in running the Rivers Large boats cannot run the River that is White River I was down to Town to day and I seen the Cars Start out for Little Rock A Great many Citizens was going to Little Rock Women ware going out there this place afords some very nice looking women it seems more like home to me than any place i have seen for sometime I am geting to like the South very well I expect that I will want to live in the South after the War if I live to see it threw the hardest looking people that I have Seen in the South is Refegees they are people that has had everything taken from them and when they come to our lines they are about gon in I have to pitty such people Especialy the women and Children that is the only class of people in the South that I can Strong Rebs as the men are Those women I cannot pitty I have seen women that there husbands ware in the Rebs Army and they ware Union Sentiment Those men ware conscripted Well I understand that it is circulated in the Iowa papers that our Regt was going for McClellen by a large majority Our Regt is for Lincoln I suppose probably if nothing hapens Mack will get between 25 or 50 votes out of about 450 men that is a doing very well for Mack I would think that our Regt was ignerent if they did not know enough to Shun any man that Expected the Nomination by the Chicago Convention that Convention made more Lincoln men then it did Mack men in the Army I cannot nor want support such Platform or any set of men but one and a

Person can hardly find a Regt in this Department but what the majority is for Lincoln If Mack had come out independent he would have run a great deal stronger but all things are working for the Better I am well and hearty at present hoping these lines will find all of you in good health Weather is cool here One or two Frosts has fallen here I must close from your loving Husband
Silas I Shearer to Elizabeth J. Shearer

Duvalls Bluff Ark
Oct the 30th 1864

Dear Wife I take the present Sabbath Morning to write you a fiew lines to inform you that I am well and hearty at present hopeing these fiew lines may find all of you well and hearty and enjoying pleasure I am Enjoying Soldiers life as well as I ever did I enjoy it the best here of any place that we have been with the Exception of Texas This place is more like home to me than any place I have been for a long time and am enjoying it very much there is nothing so Cheering as to see a Soldier full of life and fun It goes to Show that they are Enjoying themselves very much Whatever a Soldier can Enjoy themselves as I think he should do it A great many probably would differ with me I would not go in to anything bad and would not like to see anyone else go in to such masurs for pleasure Although there is a fiew that will do anything to have a little fun and what they think pleasure but I would think different I try to respect my people that is at home I do not think because I am in the Army that I can do anything I please and u will never get home I try to behave myself as though I was at home if I live I shall want to go home and I want to go home

Camp 23rd Iowa Brownesville, Ark
November the 24th, 1864

Beloved Wife I take the pleasure this Evening to write you a fiew lines in answer to two letters I received from you to day. They bear date of October the 18th and Nov the 7th I was glad to hear from you once again although I began to think that you had forgoten that there was such a being as me or that you thought it wasent worth your time to write to me but I find it is all a mistake when these letters came It has been about six weeks Since I received a letter from you untill these. You bet I was glad to hear from you again and to hear that you was all well and hearty nothing pleases me beter than to hear such news it is cheering to a soldier to get a letter from the loved ones at home if it contains but a dozen words so it is health and pleasure but I like a large letter to read A short letter is to me as a Small bit of meat is to a Dog I read it and look for more (a dog eats his meat and licks his chops for more) this is the difference between me and a Dog although I am happy to get any kind of a letter from you I donot want you to understand that I want to pick a fuss with you I cannot complain of your writing for you write as large letters as I do generaly. Well Jane I am glad to hear that Father and Mother and Benton went and returned from Indiana without any accident I am in hopes they had a happy time of it and that they enjoyed the trip very much I suppose they found Oald Hoosiey a little different than when they left it before time changes all things one way or the other I am in hopes that all of you will enjoy your selves very much this winter in the new house that Father built this fall I am glad to hear that his house was very nigh finished I think he can enjoy himself this Winter a great deal better than he has here to fore I would like to be there one night to see how you look in a new house the time is roling around when I can be at home if nothing hapens Well Jane you say that the weather is tolerable disagreeable in Iowa probably it is but I would not think so probably you would not if you was here in my place a fiew weeks. This is the greatest Country for Cold rains I ever seen it has rained more than half of the time since we came up White River We have nothing but Dog Tents as well call them (Shelter Tents properly named) it goes a little tuff when we move and first go in to camp when we camp and likely to stay a week or so we go to work rig us up a little shanty of logs and slabs that we cut in the Timber and cover it with our tents After we get our Shanty finished and a fire place in it then we can keep comfortable while we get to Stay in but we have to go on duty when our time comes rain or Shine nothing but Sickness prevents a person from going on duty when he is with the <u>Co</u> if he is not on daily duty it has been very disagreeable Since we have been here It raines three or four days and then clears up coald The country is so very flat here that the water cannot run off The last time I was on Picket we had to wade the water to get to the posts and then could hardly find ground enough to quarter six men two Corporals and One Sarg! but as luck would have it .. it did not rain but little while I was out I expect to be on duty to morrow if nothing hapens and it looks very much like rain I come on duty every fifth or Sixth day Since we came up the River duty has been heavey on us Since we came up the River I have been on Picket every time that I have been detailed for the last two months but do not grumble in the least I will write so more Silas Shearer to Elizabeth Shearer

Camp Nigh Brownesville Ark
Sat Nov the 12th 1864

Dear Companion I take the present opportunity of writing you a fiew lines to let you know that I am well at present and I Sincerely hope these fiew lines will find all of you well and hearty Well Jane I hardly know what to write It has been over a month Since I received a letter from you The last letter I received from you was dated Sept. the 25th It came to me Octs the 10th this was the last letter I received from you The mail has come to the Regt and the boys would get letters but none would come for me and I cannot tell what is the cause Sometimes I think the is Something the matter at Home and then again I think they get Miss layed probably you have fogot to write to me because I did not write to you for nigh four weeks Well a Soldier in the Army has a very poor chance to write at the best and Sometimes they have know chance to write at all and the people at home can write when ever they feel like it Us Soldiers has to write when ever we can but I will drop this thinking I will get a letter soon Well I must say that we got a chance to vote last Tuesday and a Wednesday morning we marched for this place we march it in one day and a half we marched in sight of the R Road the grater part of the way it had been raining for three or four days before we marched We marched threw a prairie with the exception of two miles The prairie was very level and the water lying on the top of the ground Consequentially we waded about Six miles We got threw but a great many of the boys felt pretty oald and I felt pretty oald and I felt as Oald as the Oaldes of them. I cannot stand marching very well anyway and marching threw water uses me up for a fiew days We are now in Camp Nigh Brownsville about two miles and a half from the R. Road Station how long we will stay here I cannot tell Well I must tell you how the Election went as far as I know and then close Our Regt stood 362 for Lincoln 38 for McClellen the 20th Iowa stands for Lincoln a large majority McClellen only 24 the 35th Wisconsin majority for Lincoln 32 Thirty two is the majority that Lincoln got in that Regt this is our Brigade the 12 Michigan Twelve Hundred strong went 900 for Lincoln and 300 for McCellen that is all I heard of on the account of us leaving the next morning You know where I am and how I am geting along when this letter was written so I will close Yours as Every Silas I. Shearer to Elizabeth J. Shearer

Duvalls Bluff Ark
Dec the 6th 64

Dear Jane I seat myself to write you a fiew lines to inform you that I am well and hearty at present. I received a letter from you yesterday the 5th it bear date Nov the 25th it came threw in a very short time I received a letter from you about a week ago It was an oald letter bringing some of the back news. These is two of you letters out yet one of them is two months oald and the other one is the one behind the letter I received yesterday. Probably you would like to know how I can tell when a letter is back. this is the way I tell. You Say that you write every week or ten days and I set down the date of every letter and the time I receive them. Therefore I can tell when a letter is missing I have never failed yet. Probably the one letter was strayed so far that I will never get it. Well Jane I was glad to hear that you was all well and hearty You say that clothing is very high That it costs so much to cloth you and the two children I do not know what you would think if you had a half a dozen children to cloth and to maintain and only the wages of a Soldiers to do it with as a great many does. I want you to cloth yourself and sweet children comfortable if it takes One hundred Dollars but you think to much of money to but so much clothing I want you to keep yourself and children comfortable I am glad to hear that you had bought two Sheep if you can get two or three more I want you to do it then you will have enough to make you clothing and it will be a great deal better than to buy clothing They will not be very much bother to you untill I get home if I am so lucky as to get home. I expect Sheep is very hard to get at present All I have to say is to do the best you can and you will please me Well Jane we have come back from Brownesville and I am well pleased with the exchange It was muddy all the time we ware there. The ground is rowling here on the River We have a very nice Camp here we moved in to houses that the 46th Ill built The Houses is about fourteen feet square covered with boards It is the best quarters that we have had since we left St. Louis There is hopes of our staying here all Winter I would as soon stay here all Winter as anyplace I know unless it is New Orleans I would rather stop there in Winter than any place I know of My reason for that is because it is not so Cold We have to Drill considerable here but that is not a going to hurt any body. We left Brownsville the 30th of Nov and came here the 1st of Dec Our quarters has been Inspected nigh every day that we have been here I suppose it is to see whether we live like Hogs or Humans It has been so long since we have lived in houses that they think we do not know how to keep them clean and nice We are very nicely fixed if we had (As the Col told two of our Boys) a woman a piece then we would think we are in Paradise Our Major went home this last fall and married a girl he brought her to the Regt with him She is here now She is a very good looking woman This place is improveing very fast To be here in Dixy Northern people has came here and gon in to business of some kind or other I suppose we will have Battallion Drill this afternoon so I will stop writing.

Well Jane you Said that you had rented our place to Uncle Pery it is all right as far as I am conserned So it is taken care of and the young Timber is not Destroid is all that I care about I think that he will not do that I expect that Uncle Pery has bought the piece of land that I wanted but that is all right. You Spoke of buying some Timber or rather that Timber could be bought tolerable reasonable Well I will say this if you cannot sell the piece of land we have got for 250.00 dollars or as much as you can get for it you can if you will buy 3 or 5 acres of Timber if it is tolerable good if the Timber is not very good have nothing to do with it I would rather draw my Timber as far again if I can get good Timber I would rather Sell my land unless there is some chance of geting that Forty of Fattish lying West of myne but you know how things are going You can tell better what to do or you Pap can if you cant If I was at home I could tell in a minute what to do I wont take less than Two Hundred and Fifty for the land Do the best you can in Timber and I will be pleased I was preparing to buy that piece of land joining the grove on the North The piece we could see so plain from you paps house It was very high ground and Timber on the North-West of it I presume that is the piece Uncle Pery has bought If I had the Forty West of mine I would not sell on know consideration. I do not expect you can sell it for what I ask for it. It is such a nice place for winter is the reason I like it I expect it will be imposible to buy that of Fattish I would give more for that Forty than any Wild prairie that I know of the same amount of Acres that I would have as much land as I want and then I would be satisfied to live there You need not tell Fattish this or he would ask a Thousand Dollars for it Well Jane the talk is now that we will not stay here long (Well I must stop for Supper I wish I could take supper with you to night Well I have had my Supper and have been detailed for Regt Comisary Guard but I do not report untill in the morning The war is certainly a going to come to an end The boys say that the Commander is a feared to risk me of Picket if they could not find something to run a fellow about they would dye if they get a rig on any of the Boys they donot know when to stop)

It is reported that we are to go to the Shanandoe Valey I suppose we have to report to Memphis whether we go any farther or not Two Regt of our Brigade was at the Bluffs. The Adjutant General came from there the other day and he said that the Two Regt had embarked for Memphis I think we will go soon for we are a lost Brigade here That is what makes me think we will leave Ark soon If we do not leave soon I will think we will stay all Winter You wrote to me that you had some notion of going down to Mothers with Uncle Weslys Why did you knot go It would have pleased Mother to have you come Well Jane I got a letter from Elias the other day He was well the time he wrote He said he had received a letter from you the day before He wrote if you hear anything from Andrew I want you to let me know it. I have written to you every week or ten days since we came in off of the Atchafalaya the 10th of Oct Retreat is played by the Band now it is geting dark So I must Stop writing Well Jenna this is the 25th It is raining and I am on Guard but I need not be in the rain very much.

If nothing hapens Dave Perin and I are going to Little Rock tomorrow Well Jane I must say without braging that I can Sew and make close and repare them as well as the most of the fair sex I made me a vest and the boys say it is hard to beat for the first if I live to get home you will be know where with me probably you think I am blowing but I am not I must close for this time hoping to get an answer soon I remain you affectionate Husband S. I. Shearer to E. J. Shearer

Well Jane I will try and write a fiew more lines We had Brigade Drill this After-noon on the Prairie It is about one mile from our Camp It is a Splendid Sight to see a lot of Troops Drilling on the Prairie The prairie is very level and nice for Troops to Drill on. I suppose we will have to Drill every day that the weather is favorable unless we are on fatigue I like to Drill when it is Battallion or Brigade Drill if the weather is not to warm The weather is very nice and favorable for Drilling but Company Drill I dislike but we have to keep that up once a day while we stay here. Well Jane I wrote to you in my last letter that Dave Perin and I was going to Little Rock We went up to Little Rock on the morning train andthe train following us ran off of the track Six miles of Little Rock. A yoke of Cattle was on the track and when the train came to them instead of them runing off of the track they run up the track and came to a bridge They fell threw. it being dark the cars run on to them Tore the Bridge down Threw the Engine and Tender and seven cars off and completely smashed them to pieces The Engine and Tender run across the bridge and fell off on the right hand side of the road the other cars went off on the right hand side of the road and the other cars went off on the left side of the water. The road and Bridge was Eight and Ten feet high Two flat cars was all that stayed on the road The other cars and engine was upside down one or two soldiers was killed dead and several badly hurt. One Lieut had one arm and both legs broken and was hurt in the breast and head He was not expected to live. An Irish woman and girl 12 or 14 years oald a little boy 8 or 10 years oald was taken here Husband a Corps to Little Rock to bury him. The flesh on the woman thigh was cut off of the bone to her knee the bone was not broken The little girl had her foot and ancle mashed and was fast so she couldnot get loos untill helped Some of the boys that helped the girl out said that the girl said for them to help her ma out and then they could help her out they said she never shed a tier She stood it like a Soldier. The little boy had his leg broken The woomen was not expected to live I seen where they had to cut the people out of the cars where they war fast The Conducter said that it was a wonder that any boddy excaped Five men was on the Engine and no one of them hurt The Cars was loaded with Comisearies principly pork and flour I have heard a great deal of talk of Smashup on the RR and if this is the way they smash up I do not want to be on them when it occurs. I never seen things smashed up so bad in my life Dave and I stoped at Little Rock untill our pass run out and come to the conclusion we would have to get down some way We got on a flat car that was runing out and stoped an hour or two and an Engine and a flat was there and they run to Brownesville so we hoped aboard We got back safe The road was repaired in three or four days Little Rock is a nice town business seems to be going on very brisk I seen Sam Thompson he got to the 40th Iowa the night before we got there He said that he had seen you just before he left home He was up there and he said I had a very smart boy. I expect he will be big by the time I get home I also seen Joseph Runyon He was not very well I seen several of my oald School mates in the 36th Iowa I must close for it is geting late The boys are all in bed and I expect you are too so no more at present Your affectionate Husband S I Shearer to E. J. Shearer

Duvalls Bluff Ark
Dec the 15th 1864

Dear Jane, I embrace the present opportunity to write you a fiew lines to let you know that I am well and hearty, and full of fun. I sincerely hope these fiew lines may find you and the children and connection all well. Well Jane we are here at Duvalls Bluff yet, enjoying our selves the best we have since we have been in the Service, although we have to work on Fortifycation every three or four days, and have to drill every day that the weather is favorable, but we have comfortable quarters to go to, that is a great cosolation to a soldier. I was working this fore noon the squad I was with went to the Prairie to cut Sod for the Fort, we was on the outside of the Picket line, we had a easy job, twenty of us cut sod and loaded four teams twice and then went in, I understand that there is three Forts yet to build here after this one is finished. If we stay here we will have to build or help build them. We have to drill twice a day, Company drill in the forenoon, and Battallion or Brigade drill in the afternoon, the boys growel considerable because they have to drill, but it good for our health. We drill on the Prairie, it is a nice place for Brigade drill. Company drill does not amount to very much. Well Jennie we have had some very good weather here. Three or four days ago it was very cool. Ice was an inch and a half thick, the ground was frozen three or four inchs deep, that was the 11th and 12th of this month. Probably you may think it was not very cold, I thought it was it was as cold to us here as it is in Iowa, I donot know what I will do if I live to get out of the service it will be so cold in Iowa that I will almost feeze to death. A persons blood gets very thin here in the

South. Cold weather goes very hard with a person here, and we have to be on guard duty wet or dry, cold or warm, we have to go out and watch, while those in Camp sleep, I haven't been on guard since the 28th of last month. Guard duty is not very hard on us at present that does not fret me. Well Jane I seen Dek Margset this morning I hardly knew him he looks so much better than he did at home. well I am geting my letter all mixed together so here she goes, deserters come in here every fiew days, that are from Prices Army, they say that Prices men are considerably scattered and are deserting him as fast as they can, everything is quiet on this side Bushwhacking is very nigh dried up on this side. We haven't been bothered with them since we came up the River how long it will last I cannot tell, they say they are not agoing to stand another campain on this side They are whiped and are willing to give it up, we only have there word for it Well Jane it is very warm tonight. it is now after ten Oclock and I must go to bed. I wish I was at home to go to bed so good night.

(Newspaper Clipping attached)
ATTENTION LADIES A young man in the service of Uncle Sam, Twenty four years old, neither handsome or rich, but fond of fun. is desirous of corresponding with a limited number of LOYAL young ladies in Iowa. "Object" improvement and pastime for some of the many unoccupied hours consequent to camp life. All Correspondence strictly confidential.

Address   Frank C_____   Co K 23rd Iowa volunteers via New Orleans La

Duvalls Bluff Ark
December the 25th, 1864

Dear Wife I seat myself this afternoon to write you a fiew lines in answer to a letter that I received the 21st It bears date Dec the 3rd I was pleased to hear from you again but was sorrow to hear that the children had the sore eyes. I hope that they will be well of that disease soon, sore eyes is very painful and disagreeable and it is injurious to the eyes, a persons eyes is never as good after having the sore as before. Well Jane I will tell you the reason that I did not answer your letter before this. I want on Picket the next morning and after I came in I had considerable of sewing to do, I was changeing the pockets and sewing stripes of the legs of pants so I did not get time to write untill to day Well Jane this is Christmas so the boys say and it only comes once a year. Taking all things in to consideration, we thought we would have a little Spree. We took our Spree last night and finished today with an Oyster dinner. I feel alright now but to tell the truth of the business I was a little foxy. This is the first Spree that I have had since I have been in the Service and I intend it to be the last one, probably some one will write home concerning it, so I thought I would be the first to write it. A Soldier sees a great deal of hard times and I cannot blame them for having a good time once and a while and I dont think that you will blame me. We have had some very cold weather here the last time that I was on Picket it was clear and cold one of these sneeking cold nights but it has moderated and to day it is trying to rain. It is very muddy and will remain so threw the winter I presume. Our Brigade has to furnish guards on Boats that runes to Little Rock. I understand that the last detail was a going to Fort Smith It is on the Ark River on the line between Ark and the Indian Territory. The Boats that goes from here runes down White River To the Mississippi and down the Miss as far as Napoleon then up the Ark River to these points above mentioned. If you had a war map you could see where those places are that I mention It would be a great satisfaction to you. I wanted to go on that detail that is to go to Fort Smith but I hapened to be the first on detail and I was put on Picket and Sommers went up the River. This is generaly the case if there is any detail that I would like to go on I get something else to do. I presume it will be cold running up there on the Boats but that is a Country that I always wanted to see. Well Jane I am in hopes you will enjoy this Chritmas very much I would like to be at Home with you to day but as it is I cannot I am enjoying it the best I can I am in hopes you are doing the same Well Jane I hardly know what to write. Downes is lying on the bed as usual Pat Hernon is writing as I am doing Jerry Stalb is fixing some strips for his pants I must close write when you can and I will waite untill I get them No more at present from you affection Husband S I Shearer to E. J. Shearer

Duvalls Bluff, Ark
January the 1st 1865

Dear Wife I seat myself this pleasant Sunday morning to answer your letter that I received the 29th of last month. I received a letter from Jake Crouch the same time that I received from you The reason I did not answer your letter before this I was helping make out the Muster Roll that taken two days and yesterday we had to Muster, we had monthly inspection before we was mustered and in the afternoon we maid a floor and a dore to our House that taken us untill after dark. You see that I had know time to write to you untill this morning and I thought I would write a fiew lines I am well at present and enjoying soldiers life very much and I hope these fiew lines may find you and the Children and connection all well and enjoying and enjoying New Years very much. I wish all of you a happy New Year. Well Jane I was pleased to hear from you again and that the Children eyes are geting better Youre letter bear date of Dec the 12th I presume you have very cold weather in Iowa We have tolerable Cold weather here in Ark but it is not to be compared with Iowa but it is very cold to us, Well Jane you came to the point once when you said that they was Thousands around me but I was lonesom for all that unless I could get letters from home, so I am, I can enjoy myself more in reading a letter from you than any thing else I go at I must stop for Inspection Well we are threw with Company Inspection for this morning it revives me to get a letter from home Letters from dear ones at home are consoling to soldiers, it is the greatest enjoyment of a Soldiers life to read a letter from a Dear Wife, Father or Mother Brother or Sister it is cheering to a soldier I do believe it keeps a great many from going to destruction You said in your letter that it had been some time since you had a letter from me It had been a week since you got a letter You may think that a long time if I get a letter every two weeks I think I am doing well If I got a letter once a month it would not stop my writing for I love to write to you You direction is right it does not matter whether Cairo is on the letter or not. Well Jane you said that Aunt Sarah had some new dresses It seems as though they ware very nice Well Jane I want you to get dress between now and the time I get home if I am permitted to go home and I want you to have it ready to wear when my time is out Well Jane Cap sayes he is very much oblige to hear of Josephine health and where abouts. Well I hardly know what to write. The boys are out shooting at targets They keep up considerable of noise Well Jane we have to put on considerable of stile since we came here We have to have our boots blacked our close brushed clean every thing neet as the boys call it regular studhorse style I must close for this time no more at present Your loving Husband Silas I Shearer to Elizabeth J. Shearer

Duvalls Bluff Ark
January the 3rd 1865

Dear Wife I take the present opportunity to write you a fiew lines again, to let you know that I am well at present and I hope that these fiew lines will find you well when they arrive. Well Jennie I wrote you a letter the first day of the month but we are under Marching Orders or rather have orders to Embark for New Orleans but I donot know how soon we will go We probably will go in a day or two, we may get orders to pak up before night. The Pickets have been relieved, by that I think we will go soon. I would like to go the New Orleans if we could get to stay there, some say we are a going there to do Provo duty and some say we are to go to Mobiel, for my part I would rather stop at New Orleans. The three best Regt of our Brigade is to do so I understand, our Regt and the 20th Iowa dnt the 37th Ill is the three Regt that is to go, the other Regts is to stay here so reports say. We are geting things fixed so we could live like humans, but that is generaly the way when a Regt gets fixed so as they can live and see a little pleasure they have to leave and go some wheres else. I would truly give up this place for New Orleans if we could stay there a while Some how or other I dont think we will stop there any length of time. I always like the looks of New Orleans and would have been satisfied to stay there from the first time I seen the place. I believe it is the healthiest City in the South and a person sees something new every day that gives him pleasure and satisfaction and that is what passes time for a Soldier. I have seen more pleasure since we came up White River than I did all last summer we were at Morganzia Bend all last summer and all that we seen was Soldiers, no improvement or anything else going on, up here everything is lively it seems as though people was trying to live Well Jennie this is Jan and it is very warm and pleasant the ground was frozen but very little last night in the holows was all the plac I seen frooze, and that very slightly but we need such weather here. In Iowa I presume you have very cold weather, it is the time of the year for to be cold, if we get to New Orleans we will not see as Cold Weather as we have seen here. our Winter is very nigh two thirds past. We have afloor two windows and a very good Batten door to our House, and yesterday we repared the Jams and Back Wall and built a new Chimney and now we have to leave it.

Well Jennie probably I will not get a chance to write to you again before I get to our journeys end If that should be the case I dont want you to stop writing, you are where you can get plenty of stamps and I want you to write to me often I dont care if you write every day or two You cant spend money any better. The longer I am away from you the dearer you and Children seem to me and a letter is a token of your love, it is hardly nine months untill my time is out and it seems a long time yet. I remember when the 8th Ind had but 8 or 9 months to serve I thought it was but a short time then Jennie much kiss them for me and that care of them. I would like to see you and the darlings very much Write often my dear and give me the general newes I presume we will be to our Journies end before you get this. Firm is the ring that has no Spring. Write often and I will do the same my Queen. Your loving Husband SIS to EJS

Jan the 4th 1865

Dear Wife I take the present opportunity to write you a fiew lines to let you know that I am well at present and I hope these fiew line may find all of you well and hearty, and enjoying pleasure. Well Jane I and J H Stall has expressed some clothing by Adams Express Co They will come to Nevada if they go threw, Jerry Stalls Clothing is on top. You will find a division made with paper and Jerrys clothing is on the top of the paper. Jerry sent an over coat dress coat one blouce one pair of drawers, and these you will first come too, and then you will come to the aboved named paper, then you will take the paper off and then you will come to my clothing. Now I will describe my clothing One over coat one dress coat one Blouce two shirts too drawers. Now Jane this Blouce is for you, it makes a nice coat for a woman to ware around home in the Winter time. Jerry sent his Blouce for the same purpose that I did, now Jane you must mark Jerrys clothing so as you will know them and take good care of them untill we get home. You pay for the Box and write what it cost and Jerry and I will make it all right. I and Jerry had clothing enough to fill that box and he had no one to send with to Marshalltown, so he sent his clothing with myself for you to take care of and I want you to take care of it as though they were myne. I told him that you would take care of them and you must do it.

And one pair of Trowsers for me, these Trowsers have there pockets remodeeled but I did not do it. I traided for them and then I thought I would send them home and keep the pair I fixed for they ware a great deal nicer. That is about the pockets, they are the same kind of trowsers other ways. I intended to send some cloth for you to fix the pockets over Now if you get these things I want you to write immediately whether you get the clothing I described This box will come in your Paps name pay him for the trouble I put him to, Well Jane we are here in the mud yet and not it is very nigh to our arms and still gets worse but thank fortune we are a going to get out of it, whether we will better ourselves or not, we got Orders last night to be ready to go a board of a Propeller at any minute I understand that we are to go to Mobiel point. If we get on a Propeller we are a going to cross the Salt Water to Alabamma. Well Jane we are not paid yet and if we leave here I see but little prospect of being paid soon. If we are not paid soon and you have money enough to do you untill I get home. I dont know as I shall have any untill I get home and still depend on you for Stamps. I expect it will be forward to the place we are in when we are paid whether I draw or not. Well Jane I have not heard from Heaths since your Paps got back. Your affectionate Husband S I Shearer to E. J. Shearer

Duvalls Bluff Ark
Jan the 5 1865

Dear Wife I take the present opportunity to write you a fiew lines in answer to a letter that I received from you today It bear date December the 26th It came threw in seven or eight days I was very much pleased to hear from you again. I feel as proud as a bird set free when I get a letter from you I donot seen any thing that pleases me better than a letter writen by you dear hand If you knew how glad

I am when I get a letter from you you would write every day or two. I was in another tent or house when your letter came. You bet I did not stay there long I soon went in to see who the letter was from When I found out it was from you it wasent long untill I found out what was in it Well Jane you said that you had a Turkey roast at Christmas Well I am in hopes you enjoyed yourself very much I would like to been there and taken Christmas with you Probably you could enjoyed your self better I know I could enjoyed myself a great deal better with you. Well Jane you say that you wish I was at home so I could go to that good Templers meeting. Well as far as being at home I would not object but more than likely I would not gone to that meeting I could enjoy myself better at home if I had been there If I was young and wanted to spree a round that it would suit me but as I am it does not. Now you need not think that I am throwing any slurs to you or the Lodge for I believe in everybody a doing as they like Well you said that the Timber was all gon that was any account and that you was not a going to buy any of it I am glad to hear it for I can get Timber of Edward Thayer almost as cheap as you can get that in the grove and it is a great deal better it lays in the grove not far from the oald man Thayers place. If I knew how the Timber lay I would buy five or Ten acres, but I guess I will let it slide untill I get home Then I can choose for myself, if I had 40 acres of Prairie to that 40 I would not sell it would just suit me, and when I am pleased then I am satisfied Well you said you had a new dress and you wished I was at home so I could make it for you because I was such a good sewer. I fear you are a sluring me how someever there is other things that I can make for you a great deal easier and better than I can a dress and take more delight in it but if I was at home aand you could not make the dress I could make it. Well Jane I received a letter from Mother today it was dated Dec the 22nd She was well when she wrote but she said that Elias was taken Prisioner He was taken the 13th of Oct and the last they heard of him he was down in Florida He was well she said that Andrew was taken the 21st and 22nd of August. They heard from him threw a Soldier that was taken at the same time This Soldier was exchanged he said that Andrew was well Mother has bad luck with her boys, out of five two were killed, two taken Prisioner and one yet not in Rebles hand but the Lord only knowes how soon he might be a Prisioner or under the sod by the Rebles Ball. Mother sayes she wants me to write often to her for I am the only boy that can write to her at present. I can not help but feel for mother.

Part of another -starts page 5
January 1865

Well Jane today is the 21st and I though that I would write a fiew lines. I am off of guard and it has stoped raining, but it is partialy cloudy. it rained all day yesterday and last night, this morning about four Oclock it Stoped raining and today the Sun Shines a part of the time. when it does Shine it is very hot, Well Jane gardens look very nice here, at this time I suppose that is a head of you there is a garden by our Camp and it looks very nice. Onions and such vegetables that will Stand hard weather is growing nice. Union people live here and the boys donot bother. The frogs is holloring very lively, if I should come South I would come to LA as clost to Carlton or New Orleans as I could get. I can remember when I was at home that it was said that New Orleans was a very unhealthy place and that people from the North couldnot live here it was preached to me so much that I thought it was so, but I find it a mistake. I believe that New Orleans is as healthy a City as there is in the South. I would as soon risk it as any that I know and it is a great place to make money Wages is very high here, and I might say everything else in proportion but at the same time I like to be where I can raise Corn Wheat Potatoes and such things and have plenty of them, therefore I will have to take the North for it. I think I can be satisfied to live in Iowa contented with my Dear little family if I am permitted to get out of the Service alive. Well Jane I understand that the money has come to New Orleans to pay our Brigade but I have not heard how soon we will get it but I suppose you have money by you yet I must close for this time no more at present your affectionate Husband S. I. Shearer to E. J. Shearer

Well Elizabeth Jane, I had brought my letter to a close, as I was a finising it the Mail came to our Regt and behold two letters came to me. one was from my Jane. it was dated Jan the 8th and arrived this after noon the 21st I was as eager to read this letter as I was the one I got night before last. The other letter that I got today was from Mary and Amy Shearer they was all well when they wrote. Mary said that she had not a letter from Cousin Jane for a long time and she knew not the cause of it. She said when I wrote to you to tell you to write to her, now and then, well Jane I am glad to hear that you have such nice weather in Iowa. I think it is time you have a nice pleasant Winter. The other two winters that I have been gon was very cold. you probably can enjoy yourself this Winter better than usual. We seen some tolerable cool weather in Ark and disagreeable weather here. About the time you spoke of the weather being so nice with you in Iowa, it was with us rainy and disagreeable a fiew days least and cold, we ware on the boat a part of that time Well Jane Oald Maguett rather played off on you, but it was a fine thing that you had not payed your Money for them or else Sheep Money and all would have been gon. Well Jane you need not trouble yourself about me for I will try and get along the best way I can. It is a hard place for a person to be sick in the Army, but I think I have had my Sickness the first year that I was out, although I may see considerable of Sickness yet, before my time is out when a Soldier has his sickness the fore part of his term and gets well he is generaly very apt to be hearty the remainder of his time I must close this, your affectionate Husband, S. I. Shearer to E. J. Shearer

"Uncle Sam's Farm"

Of all the mighty nations in the East or in the West
Oh this glorious Yankee nation is the greatest and the best
We have room for all creation and our banner is unfurled
Here is a general invitation to the people of the World
Chorous
Come along Come Along make no delay
Come from every nation come from every way
Our land is broad enough - dont be alarmed
For Uncle Sam is rich enough to give us all a farm

St. Lawrence markes our Northern as fast her waters flow
And the Rio Grand our Southern bound way down to Mexico
From the great Atlantic Ochean where the Sun begins to dawn
Leaps across the Roca Mountains away to Oregon
Chorous
The South may raise the Cotton and the West the Corn and Pork
New England manufactures Shall do up the finer work
For the deep and flowing waterfalls that course along our hills
Are just the thing for washing Sheep and driveing Cotton Mills
Chorous
Our fathers gave us liberty but little did they dream
The grand results that flow along this mighty age of Steam
For our mountains lakes and rivers are all a blaze of fire
And we send our news by lightning on the telegraphic wire
Chorous
Yes we are bound to beat the nations for our Moto's go ahead
And we'll tell the foreign paupers that our people are well fed
For the nations must remember that Uncle Sam is not a fool
For the people do the voting and the children go to School
Chorous

Kennerville LA
Jan the 28th 1865

Dear Wife I seat myself to write you a fiew lines to let you know that I am well at present and I sincerely hope that these fiew lines may find all of you well and hearty. Well Jane I thought I would write you a fiew lines this Evening We are still here in the mud and know prospect of geting away yet. It has been cold rainy and is disagreeable ever since we have been here and know prospects of geting any better yet It is cold cloudy and disagreeable and prospects of rain Well Jane I am agoing to send you a Co Reccord when it comes I want you to be careful in opening it, in the first place you must push the wooden roll out of the inside before you take the rapper off After taken the wood out then you can get the rolls without injuring it. I want you to have a frame and glass for it and that before you get it dirty. If you get it in a frame I would not take ten dollars for it. If you get it let me know it Be carefull when you open it. I received a letter from mother today. They were all well she said that Andy was at Andersonville GA You must excuse me for not writing more for it is so cold and disagreeable that I can hardly write. yours as ever S I Shearer to E. J. Shearer

Kennerville La
Jan the 31st 1865

Dear Wife I seat myself this afternoon to write you a fiew lines to let you know that I am well and hearty and I hope that these fiew lines may find all of you well and hearty and enjoying hapiness. I received a letter from you yesterday it bare date Jan the 14th I was glad to hear from you again. Your letter was read with pleasure and I was glad to hear that you and family and connection was well. You say that colds are very bad in Iowa, well that is not very dangerous, unless it is so severer that it terminates in or contracts some other disease. Colds is not uncomen in this part of the country but not so severe as in the North. I have had several colds since I have been in the Army but they were very light. They did not hurt me. The South is a better country for a person that has weak lungs or a consumtive person has better health in the South than they do in the North, but it is said that my lungs is very strong again. They ware considerable affected after I got over the meazles, but I thought for a long time that they ware too badly injured to get well again. I believe that I am stronghter at present than I have been since I was sick at Uncles Perrys, but I think at the present time that I will never live in the South after I get out of the Army, Although circumstances alters cases for the present I have enough of the South. Well Jane I am on Commissary Guard again but it not raining at the present time but it is cloudy and perhaps will rain before it cleares up, but winter will soon be over here and then we will have some nice weather and I will be glad to see it. I would rather Soldier in warm weather than in cold weather. Well Jane you said that you would send me a box of provisions if I thought it would get threw. Well Jane my advice to you is not to send it. I have several reasons for it, first place we are not shure to remain in one place very long, and probably we will have to run threw the country, and probably I never would get it, and then it costs considerable to get a box to me and I can get a long very well with out it if I keep my health and then five dollars would be saved. I have seen provisions sent to Regt and there was know care taken of the boxes and they get wet and the provisions ware all spoiled. I would like very well to have some those things that you mentioned but I will wait untill I get home, then I can take some pleasure in eating them. I think you had better not send the box.

Well Jane the talk is now that we will go below New Orleans to Jackson Barracks. That is where Jackson fought the battle of New Orleans it is in the Surburbs of the City and a very nice place. I would like to go there This is one of the most forsaking places I ever seen. Well Jane I want you to pay that note off in money that Dan Swarm has against me if you can do it although I did not get all the property that I bought of him. If you can square the note well and good and if not wait untill I get home. The note calls for twelve dolars. Well Jane there is some talk of consolidating our Regt If it is consolidaed there will be considerable of reducing among the non Commissioned Officers but according to the Order from the War Department, the Non Commish shall be mustered out, the order is this, when a Regt Shall be consolidated. The Corps or Division Comander shall examine the Commision and Non Commision Officers and take the best to fill the vacancies or take those that are the most competent to fill such places and the over plus of Commision and Non Commision officers shall be mustered out, but this is seldom done. I think it is as the Col says about reducing the Non Commish but the Comishened Officers are mustered out but I think a Non Commish has no more right to be mustered out than a Private has and I think the same of the Commishioned Officers, but I understand that our Coln is opposing the consolidation and we may not be consolidated. For my part I would rather not, but I guess I can stand it Seven months longer, Well Jane tell me who Abagail is working for and what she is a working at. Probably you may think I am inquisitive, but I asked for information and tell me what Regt you Cousin Shenkle has gon to if you know. I dont want you to tell me unless you know (now thats green) Well Jane write to me the price of land and whether the price is going up and down. I have some notion that if you can traid my land for Stalk or a part in Stalk and the balence in money to have you do it. I would rather have all money if you should hapen to traid it for Stalk. I want you to get young Stalk if I could get Three Hundred Dollars I could sell that I would not buy at present. I mean if I get home I would rent for a while untill I could see a good chance but you are at home and you can tell best what to do. Your Pap could tell whether it would be best to sell or not. Downs was talking a little about buying it I must close I like the place well enough If I had a forty of Prairie. Your affectionate Husband S. I. Shearer to E. J. Shearer

Well Jane I will have to be up untill 3 OClock in the morning I go on at 9 this evening and off at 3 a.m. When I was young and runing after the girls I could be up very easy

Kennerville La
Feb the 8th 1865

Dear Wife To night I seat myself to write you a fiew lines to let you know that I am well and hearty at present and I hope that these fiew lines may find all of you well and hearty. Well Jane I received your kind and welcome letter today the 8th It bear date Jan the 22nd I was glad to hear from you again, to hear that you ware all well and hearty, that is the best news that I can hear I love to read a letter when it Sayes my dear ones at home are well. From what you say you are not lacking for company I hardly ever get a letter but that mentions some one at Paps, in adition to there folks, well time passes a great deal faster with company than with out. I am glad to hear that you have Company You do not get so lonesome, when Company comes in it is a change and things seemes more livelier. Well Jane I wish I had been at home that Sunday that you Spoke of the boys agoing a Sparking. I think we could have had as nice a time as they could, especialy Bob, if he had have taken the one that he talked of, you bet. Well Jane when I wrote to you last I said that we was under Marching Orders, so we was and are yet but we have not got away from this mud hole yet, and I cannot tell how soon we will go but I think it will be soon and I care not how soon for this is the worst place that I ever seen or ever want to see while a Soldier It is so muddy that it all most impossible to get a round. It rained for four or five days strait a long and yesterday it cleared up and it is tolerable cold, it is so cold that I can hardly write If it was to any one else I would not write to night and I would wait untill I got time. We drew our jackets the other day and they ware Cavalry Jackets and the Stripes had to come off of them and they needed some repairing. I have had all that I could do since we drew them today. I cut one over for our drummer boy and I did not get it finished and I have some more to fix when this one is done. Well Jane the Colonel informed one of the boys that he had a good thing for us if we would keep it he wants us to put on a stile He wants every man in the Regt to get themselves a pair of white gloves and he said that we would be paid off next week. Well I will put on considerable of style rather than to March if he will get us to a place where we can do it. Well Jennie I must stop for tonight for my fingers are num. I will try and finish the letter tomorrow night if nothing hapens and we dont move. Well Jane this is the 9th and I am like a snake, out sunning myself. I have got that jacket finished and now I will try and finish my letter. Well Jane I mention in my other letter about a box of clothing that I and Jerry Stall expressed to you in you Paps name they will come to Nevada. Jerry sent one over coat a Dress Coat One Blouse one Drawer These are on top my clothing is one over coat Dress coat one Blouse two Drawers Two Shirts one pair of trousers. These you will find in the bottom, you will find a layer of paper between Jerrys close and myne. I made a lid to the box and put a strap and buckle to it and if the leathers remains to the box you can very easy tell which is the top of the box and if the leathers are taken off the top of the box will be marked Army or Pilot Bread. The Blouse that you find with my clothing is for you to ware in the winter time You can put black buttons in the place of the brass ones, the Blouce that Jerry sent is for his woman. Now Jane mark Jerrys clothing so you will know them and take care of them untill we get home If it is our lot to get home. I said you would take care of them and think you will. Well Jane I sent another Blouse with some clothing that Dave Perin expressed to his wife It will have my name in the pocket, Jerry Stall sent a Blouse and a Shirt They will have his name to them he wants you to take care of them for him. Dave wrote to his wife concerning them and she will give them to you. The reason we did not send them in our box was this We hadent our jackets at the time that we expressed our clothing but we drew them the next day so we thought we would send those things with Daves if you get this clothing it will be worth 75 or 100 Dollars to me and if you dont get them it will be considerable lost but I couldnt marched with so much clothing and I would have had to throw the most of it away and I thought I would risk it on the road home, and it was a fine thing that I expressed when I did for this is a order now not to express any clothing but Overcoats. We may not have to march but little this Spring but it would not surprise me if we marched considerable yet before our time is out. Well Jane you said that you was a figuring up the time that I had to Serve yet we was mustered in to the U. S. Service the 19th day of September the 18th of this month we will have Seven months yet to serve. I have heard that it was the Order from the War Department to muster out all the 62 troops at the date of there Enlistment but I have not seen the Order. I suppose that we will be mustered out when ever Uncle Sam takes a notion to do it. Well Jane I understand that Gen A. J. Smith is coming down the river with his troops If that is the case I think we will have some marching to do, but if he is in command of the Expedition I dont care so much to take a tramp. Gen F Steel is in Command of our Corp Gen Steel may be a good commander but I like Smith the best, Oald A. J. is not a feared of the Jonnies, and his name is a terror to them and well it might be for he whipes them every time that he hitches on He hardly ever bawks and the boys that he has under him is just like himself, when ever they can get at the Rebles they are in there Glory, they think that Smith knowes it all. Well Jennie I will finish my letter with what I call imagineary stories, probably there is reality in them I hope so at any rate. Do you hear any talk of peace in Iowa It is all the talk down here among Soldiers Citizens and Editors. I have but little faith in it An extra was printed at New Orleans last evening containing good news if it is so, it seemes to think that the peace operation is very nigh certain. Blair had got back from Richmond the second time and this time he had good news but I did not hear what it was. Well Jane I wrote to you to traid that place off I am not very particular whether you do it or not It is a nice little place and it will make us a good home. Make a good traid if you traid it, if you cant keep it I must close for this time no more at present S I Shearer to E. J. Shearer

Camp Mobile Point Ala
Feb the 17th 1865

Dear Wife I take the present opportunity to write you a fiew lines to inform you that I am well and hearty at present and I hope that these fiew lines may find all of you well and hearty. Well Jane I received a letter from you today, it bear date Jan the 28th It came unexpected to me this time. The way I have been geting letters when we move it would be about a week yet before I would get a letter, but this time it did not change the run of my mail and I am very glad of it This letter was very exceptable I would be glad to get a letter every day but I donot expect it. I will have to be content with many or fiew. I was glad to hear that you and family and connection was all well and hearty, that is great satisfaction to me Well Jane we are in Oald Alabam at last. We left Kennerville the morning of the 11th and marched about three miles to the R. R. There we got on the cars and was drawen 8 miles by the Iron Horse We run this distance in 20 minutes then we got off at the Shell road oposite Greenville. We lay there untill three OClock in the Afternoon, then we marched for Lake Ponchartrain, we marched about half way on the Shell road which made it very hard on us, not used to marching on foot and the roads hard made our feet very sore. We passed threw New Orlenas to the Canal and followed it to the Lake. We got to MilneBurg on the Lake Shore at 8 OClock PM. I was on guard after we got there but was relieved the next morning on the account of the March the day before. We lay in this place untill half after five OClock PM of the 12th. We went aboard the James Battle, and at Nine OClock PM we shoved out. We passed Ft. Bike at 12 OClock in the night at one Oclock we anchored on the account of fog, at six Oclock the morning of the 13th the Anchor was raised and we run ahead We run out of Lake Ponchartrain in to lake Borgne We run in sight of Cat. Ship and Horne Islands, the wind blew tolerable hard and the Lake was tolerable rough, it began to rain about Seven Oclock PM

The wind blew so hard and the Lake rough and the night tolerable dark, so the Captain would not run threw the pass. That night at 8 Oclock PM we anchored untill half after Twelve on the 14th By this time it had stoped raning and the wind was not so high, the anchor was raised and we went on We run threw the pass where the ruins of Ft. Powel lay At Two OClock PM after runing threw this pass we got in Mobile Bay. We passed Ft. Gains half after Two PM passed Ft. Morgan at 3 Oclock PM we landed at Navy Cove at four PM about four miles above Ft. Morgan on Mobile Point we went ashore amediatly and marched about a half mile and stacked arms Cos K and C was detailed to onload the Boat. The Regt moved about one mile from where they got off of the Boat and went in Camp or where they intended to Camp for it was dark. It was nine OClock when we got the things off of the Boat and it was as dark as a stack of Black Cats, and Thundering and a heavy rain aproaching. After we got the things off of the Boat we went down where our Guns was Stacked. Our cooks had supper for us we had hardly finished our Supper when it commenced raining, We set there in the rain like drownding Chickens. Probably it rained an hour and then stoped. I had a woolen blanket and gum around me so I did not get wet. After the rain was over we spread down our bed on the Sand. We made our Bed large enough for five of us Cap McGowen slept with us. We lay there like mice, and in the morning we had Breakfast and then went to the Regt This Point is about one mile wide where we are. The Gulf is on one side Our Camp is on the Side to the Bay. The Bay has been very calm since we have been here but the Gulf is very rough and makes a great noise about it. Our Colonel is in Command of this Point He moved down to Ft. Morgan this morning. I cannot tell how long we will stay here. We may start for Mobile in a short time, although we are not where the forces lay that is to go against Mobile. Three White Regt Two Batteries One Colored Regt that landed about noon and the garrison at the Ft is about all that is here but that does not keep us from going to Mobile. I have heard that we was in a Brigad with the 20th Wis 94th Ill 60th Ind and 19th Iowa the two first named Regt are here on the Point I heard that the 19th Iowa was at Ft. Gains I seen a deserter from Mobile yesterday He left Mobile a fiew days ago He sayes that Six Thousand men is all that is in Mobile and he thinks that they will not fight very much. This is what all deserters say that comes from that place and that is a considerable many that comes in to our lines. Citizens say that the place will be easy taken. The Opinion is that they will evacuate the place when they see our move I think myself that they will not be cornered in that place, there provisions would not last long. They can see plain that if they are cornered in there that they are gon up It is said that the greater part of the Rebs in Mobile desires to be captured If such is the case they will not be hard to Capture. Well Jane I have not been to Ft. Morgan yet but if we stay here any length of time I shall go down From what I can learn it is very Strong Ft. If men Stand to there works it cannot be taken by Storm. We had monthly inspection this morning. I must close for this time no more at present. Your affectionate Husband Silas I Shearer to Elizabeth J. Shearer

128

Mobile Point Al
March the 1st 1865

Dear Wife I enjoy the present opportunity of writing you a fiew lines to inform you that I am well and hearty at present and I sincerely hope that these fiew lines may find all of you well and hearty. Well Jane I haven't received a letter from you since the 17th of Feb We have had know mail since that time or I suppose I should have had a letter from you. I cannot tell the cause of the mail not coming to us. It is a long time to get know letter but I have been at places when my mail was far a part. I expect that a great many times you have to wait two or three weeks for letters from me and you must not be alarmed if it is a longer time between letters to come than those that are passed and gon It has been rumored in Camp that it would be Forty days before mail would go North but that does not trouble me Mail will go out when we are at a place when it can. There is one thing that will keep the mail from going North and that is this. From all probabilities we will make a Campaine this Spring threw Ala and I understand that we are to take Twenty days rations with us If this is the case communication will probably be cut off, so as we cannot send any letters untill we get threw. We probably can make it in Twenty days and it may take us Forty. I do not know where our destination is or where we will come out at but if we go on a Campaine you cannot expect letters from me very often untill we get threw and then if I am alive you shall hear from me as soon as possible. You can expect the fall of Mobile or hear the news thereof every day probably it may reach you before this letter does. Well Jane I and Jerry Stall was down to Ft. Morgan last Sunday in the afternoon the 17th of Feb. This Fort was built in 1833 it is a curiosity to many persons that has not seen the Ft. It is or looks like it is impossible for Infantry to take it by a charge, if men stand to there works that are in Side. When a person is going to the Ft. it looks like a large mound in the Sand. A person can go upon the heap of sand very very easy, and when a person gets on to that behold they are not in, the inner bank of this Sand has a heavy brick wall and heavy canon on it This wall is about 12 or 15 feet high. A Storming Party could get this far very easy All that would stop them would be the belching of the Cannon, but now comes the blunt. Suppose they have the first row of cannon, they now have to jump down this wall that I have described, now they are in danger of the men that are inside shooting out of the post holes and canon that are doing the same, the storming party tries to advance or retreat but they cannot the above mentioned wall is behind them and a wall that is Twenty feet high or upwards in front you see that they will have to Surrender or all will be Killed The entrance to the outer works is about Twenty five yards long. It is an enclosure walled with brick and heavy doors to shut it up tite. The main Ft and heavy work are in the inside this second wall is fifteen feet or there abouts thick, then there is an other one in the inside of this It is the strongest Ft. I ever see. Although our gun boats damaged it considerable it has one Hundred and Sixty guns on it. A great deal many of them are Richmond guns. I must close on this paper

Silas I Shearer Our regt had apropriated 5800.46 dollars and still going

State of Alabama
March the 8th 1865

Dear Wife I take the present opportunity to write you a fiew lines to let you know that I am well at present (we have been marching today and I am so nervious I cannot write) Well Jane this is the 8th and I will try to write my letter and I hope that these fiew lines may find all of you well and hearty again. I received three letters from you the 7th They bear date as follows, February the 2nd, 12th, and 15th. It was about three weeks since I last heard from you untill the 7th. I was very much pleased to get those letters of yourn, and one of them was read with Satisfaction, but when I came to read the other one, it was sorrowful news to me, and the 3rd one still more sad. It is sorrowful news to me when I hear of those loved one that I left behind are sick, nothing gives me more dissatisfaction and uneasiness of mind than to hear such news but I was glad to hear that you was geting well. I know that our dear children will have the best of care while you can take care of them. I know you are a kind hearted affectionate and loving Mother to her children and they will not want for any thing as long as you can get it, anything that the children wants for there health I want you to get. I wish I was at home to help you take care of the children. I fear that you will expose yourself untill you are sick. I hope that the children are well eve this, I am not uneasy about the children not having care takeing of them, you will take as good care of them as though I was at home with you but my mind will not be at Ease untill I get another letter and I think probably that will be in a fiew days. A regular maile packet runs from New Orleans to Ft Gains twice or three times a week, and it is knowen where the 23rd is, and I think our maile will be regular while we stay here. Well Jane I am glad to hear that you have bought a piece of Timber and that you think it is worth the money that you paid for it, if it is as good Timber as you say, it is worth all you have paid for it. If I understand things and the reports are true, land is going up very fast but it will take a turn and I believe that the time is not far distant, one Extreme always followes another My Idia is know that I will not buy but little untill there is a change in prices. If I can get discharged as low down as Memphis I will try and get three or four Horses or mules. I can get that amount for one Hundred Dollars or by ading Twenty Five Dollars more Those that I am speaking about are Government property, and they are run down so as they are know account to the Government and they are sold to the highest bider.

A Great many of these are young Horses and Mules if I can get me a span of Mains I can raise me a good team from them. Some may laugh at the Idia but I have heard men say that they have seen good teams taken out of such places and for a very trifling sum of money. It is a great deal better to buy such at this time than to pay four or five hundred dollars for a team and probably in a year or two they would not be worth One Hundred and Fifty Dollars I think if I get home and I cannot get a team reasonable I will try and rent a place and have a team furnished me untill I can raise one to suit me. I expect it will be hard to get a place in that way I have thought that that was my best chance to get a good team. I dont want to pay all of my money out to get a team as soon as I get home. I would like to buy a lot of Sheep with it. I want you to let me know how much money you have left after buying that Timber. Well Jane I will send you some of curiosities that grow in Alabama

Camp 23rd Iowa
State of Alabama
March the 15th 1865

Beloved Wife I seat myself to write you a fiew lines to inform you that I am well and hearty at present and I hope that these fiew lines may find all of you well and hearty. Well Jane I do not know when this letter will go out for it appears to be a dificult matter for maile to go out, or to come in, and I thought that I would begin a letter and write a little every day untill I could send it out. Well Jane I never was heartier in my life than I am at present, and I hope that I will remain so untill my time is out. Well Jane our Regt and the 20th Wisconsin was on a little scout. We left here on Monday the 13th and marched up the Bay about 12 miles we got threw at 12 Oclock and stacked arms and got some coffee and at 3 PM we fell in and marched back to Shell Hill cove and Bivouck for the night. We did not move camp we did not take our Dog Tents with us. 4 1/2 Oclock the next morning it began to rain, and continued to rain very hard untill 12 in the day when it began to cease raining. This was the morning of the 14th At 9 AM we fell in and marched to Camp We arrived at Camp at 12 1/2 Oclock. I believe that I never seen it rain harder It was one continual Shower from the time it began untill we got to Camp, you bet there was not many dry threads on us when we got in Camp. We had to wade water a going out and a great deal more of it a comeing in and the fun of it was when we got in Camp it kept a drizeling rain in the afternoon that we could not dry our close or dry by the fire, but I have adopted a new method here in the Army, at least when it is cloudy, probably you would like to know how that is. I go to bed and get all the close that I can on me, this is the new method that I have adopted. Well we slaid thousands while we ware gon but did not loose on our side, but several of us got very sore fingers in the action. Probably you will be ancious to know what it was that we taken the lives of! Well it was Oysters those things that I like so much. Well now if I did not go in on them, I never went in on any thing that ware as fat and as large Oysters I every seen. Some of them was as large as a persons hand. I like to Eat such large one alive it does me so much good but I want a little vinegar on them when I eat them in that way. We had no vinegar with us so we maid supper of them and that is a most delicious dish I know of but one dish that I prefer to this, and that is raw Oysters with Salt Peper and Vinegar on them. I do not know how many of them I could eat, by the time I get one dish Shelled and Eat them, and Shell another dish and have it ready to Eat I am as hungry as ever for Oysters I do not know whether you ever eat any of those delicious little Animals (as I call them) if you did I know you like them and if you never did I know you would like them. I cannot see that this part of Alabama is worth three cents for any thing else but Oysters, although I seen a fiew peach trees and they ware in full bloom. You bet it looked nice to see fruit trees in the blow, where these trees ware it was not so much sand and the Timber was of different kinds, it was the pine the hickory the oak the magnolia and a great many other kind of Shrubery that I cannot name and I presume the farther in the Country we get the better land. The Country is very flat where we was with Cypress Swamps every fiew miles. All the Butternuts that we seen was one Deserter that came in our lines. He deserted the Reble Camp at 10 Oclock in the night and got a Small Boat and came to our lines before we cam back, he said that there was about Five Thousand Rebles Sixteen miles above the place that we was at. The rebles was on Fish River three Regt of Inft and Three of Cavalry. I presume that is the nighest force to us. A fiew scouts is seen every day or two this side. Two Hundred had been down the day before where we stoped, these are watching our movement. The Rebles may not make much of a stand at Fish River. I presume it will be owen to the force that comes against them. If our force is small and does not out number them very much they may resist stubbornly but I presume when we move we will go strong enough to drive them before us, as the wind does the Chaf, We are geting a very heavy force in this part of the Country And another force a comeing acomeing across from Batonroug. We will have a force coming from every direction against Mobile. I cannot see the hole where they will get out at. If they wait untill we begin to move. I under stand that the Rebles have been reinforced in this section of the Country, that is all for the better. By so doing we probably may Gobbel them. To take Lees Army out all the Rebles East of the Miss River combined cannot whip us to give us a good General when concentrated, our Army will be very large I under stand that General Canby will command the Expedition and General A. J. Smith will be with us. The oald 13th A C is reorganized and we belong to it and General Granger commands it at the present. He is a very common man and from his appearance but little style about him, and but little about Gen Canby and Smith. The Generals that is in this Army is very common men. Just such men as we want for the field, when an Army is at a Post or doing Garison duty then it will do to put on Style. I like to see it when it is done at the proper time and place but in the field is no place for Style. The Division that we belong too is at Ft. Barrankes in the vicinity of Pencicola. I cannot tell the reason why we are not with it we are detached for some reason. We may joing our Division soon and we may not for some time. I understand that the first Second and Eighth Iowa Cavalry is comeing across. There is some boys in the first that I used to go to School with. Oald Marguets boys is in the Regt the Eighth is the one that Andrew belongs to but I donot expect to see him with the Regt this Spring. The 10th Kansas is at Ft. Gains. I have a cousin in that Regt he enlisted in that Regt and I presume that he veterenized. Well Jane our three years is rolling around. If we live we will see each other before long. The Col says that our time will be up the 26th day of August. He sayes that the Regt was full and reported for duty at that time but I will be glad if we get out the 19th of Sept. I think if we get threw this Springs Campain that the majority of us will get home. Well Jane I am looking for a letter every day, Jane it is a dificult matter to get a letter out, if you do not get a letter from me for four or five weeks give yourself as little uneasiness about me as possible. I will close for this day. Your affectionate Husband SIS to EJS

Camp in the Field
March the 22nd 1865

Dear Wife I take the present opportunity to write you a fiew lines to inform you of my health and where abouts. I am hearty at present and I hope that these fiew lines may find all of you well and hearty. I received two letters from you, they came to me the 17th. We marched that morning and I could not answer them untill now. We marched the morning of the 17th the first days march was very pleasant but after that we got in to the Swamps and we had to build a great many bridges and that detained us very much. Our averige distance of marching after the first day was about five or six miles and yesterday we had to draw the wagons and Artillery very nigh all the way by hand. It rained night before last and yesterday in the fore noon and that maid the ground very soft. We marched yesterday morning at Eight Oclock and at Eight in the night we Bivouched for the night on Fish River. This morning we crossed over on the North side of the River and went in Camp on the left of Smiths Corps. How long we will remain here is more that I can tell. Probably we will stay here long enough to draw rations and then go ahead. This beats all States that I ever seen to march in. We have marched about Thirty miles since we started and it is a very low flat Swamp country. It is so miserable that birds will hardly live here there was but fiew people living in the country that we came threw We could hardly get any beef to Eat and the beef that we did get was so poor that it would hardly stand up long enough to shoot it but we would Eat them if we had to make supper of there loins just because they belonged to Rebles, not because we relished the beef. I am in hopes that we will come across more hogs and other forage when we march again for I am a big Eater. Our line extends about Seven miles long and more Troops coming. I think we have force enough to whip all the Rebles. This side of where this column and the one from Pencicola will form a junction and then we can whale them untill they drible like pups if our Army is rightly handled. Well Jane you seem to have very bad luck in buying property. I guess that you had better keep your money and not under take to buy anything for you are not very successful. Well Jane you bet I was glad when I heard that you and the children got Well I was very uneasy about you but the last letter relieved my mind very much. Well Jane I seen my cousin today that is in the 10th Kansas It was the first time that I have seen him since 1856 and I hardly knew him he is so very husky he was not very oald when I seen him last. Well Jane the maile goes out at 2 OClock so I will have to close. I may not get another chance to write untill after Mobile is taken and if such should be the case you need not be uneasy about me I must close for now your affectionate Husband Silas I Shearer Elizabeth J. Shearer

Camp in the Field
April the 8th, 1865

Dear Wife I take the present opportunity to write you a fiew lines to let you know where we are and how I am geting a long. I am well and hearty at present. And I hope that these fiew lines may find all of you well and hearty. Well Jane we now are Sieging the stronghold of Mobile, although we are about Ten miles from the City. When I last wrote to you we was at Fish River We lay there but a fiew days and then moved on to these Forts We had know oposition untill we got to the Rebles works with the Exception of some shells that the Rebles had planted in the road to blow us and our artilery up but it was discovered before many of our men got hurt. A fiew men and horses ware badly hurt with the shell, two deserters that came to our lines knew where the shells was planted, and they assisted our men to get all out that they could find. Our Brigade passed over the road without any damage from the Shell. We camped the night of the 26th about Two miles and a half of the Forts On the 27th we closed in on the Rebles works The 19th Iowa was in the advance of our Brigade. They got within a mile of the Fort before they met the Rebs It was about the middle of the day when they began to Skirmish with the Jonnies (by this time it was a raining) the 20th Wis threw up the first breastwork. After this was complete our Regt advanced several Hundred yards in front of this work (the 19th had driven the Rebs back) we threw up works in plane view of the Fort and Sharpshooters. The balls whistled about us considerable but fortunately none of us was hurt that night, we lay behind these works all night, the next morning we relieved the 20th Wis on the Skirmish line (the 20th had relieved the 19th in the Evening) and before night we was in a half mile of the Fort. We fought them there one way, behind logs stumps and any thing that would shield us from the Rebles ball. In the evening we was geting so nigh the top of the hill that we began to go fer and by morning we had tolerable good rifle pits It was laughable to see the blew coats behind the logs and stumps. They would shoot a while and then we could see them run for another log or stump. I fired considerable over a Hundred rounds at the Jonnies that day. We was on the skirmish line Twenty Four hours band then was relieved Twenty four, we go in the Rifle pits every Twenty Four hours. We have been under fire ever since the 27th of March. One olad Jonnie shot at me twice yesterday Evening, but a pole that was laying on the top of our works stoped them both. I was standing clost to a port hole A gawking at the Rebles works when one of the balls struck and threw the dirt in my face and Eyes Some of the boys for their development yelled out Sile get away from there you will draw there fire. The Lieut Colonel laughed and the joke passed on but I got out of rainge of that hole. I havent been struck yet, but Charley Town and I came very nigh geting struck by a piece of a shell The piece of Shell would weigh about three pound. Although the balls has whistled around my head considerable We have not had a man killed in the Regt since we came here and only one to die of a wound and we have had but fiew wounded in the Regt We have not had a man of our Co hurt yet we have been very lucky so far. We have found three or four dead Rebles that was killed and left lying on the ground. We are geting a great many heavy guns planted to bear on the Rebles Fort. Our Batteries opend the other Evening on the Rebles have four or five Forts here Fort McCullock Fort Savage and Fort Spanish the others I cannot name Fort Spanish was built by the Spanish when settling this country. Our Brig is on the left, a resting on the Bay (Mobile) and operating against Fort McCullock. The Rebs dont use many heavy guns They opened on us yesterday with two guns thinking to knock our Breast works down but they only got four Shot at us, our guns opened on them and they had to hide there guns. General Steel has set Siege to Blakely, he is about six miles from our right. There was as heavy canonading in that direction last night and this morning as I have ever heard. What the consequence is I do not know. Some of Gen Thomas Cavalry has came threw, Thomas has Captured Selma without a Struggle he captured Eight Thousand prisoners Two Month provision for his Army, two or three large foundries and Shot Factories, he made a clean thing of it That place is a death blow to Mobile the whole thing will be captured and all that is wanted to do it in is time. Thomas and Canby is working to get here and if they work it right they will make a big thing of it. I have heard that the Rebles force about Mobile is about 35,000 men, and they have a great many places to hold so it devides there forces. The Rebles at this place have their Supplies cut off at present, and if we can keep it cut off we will have them in two or three weeks. The Rebs have a Gun Boat or two here and they cannot get out. Gen A. J. Smith is on the right and he has ten 32 pound Parot Guns and they command the Chanel. The Reble Boat under took to dislodge this Battery but she was glad to get out of range of these Guns and let them alone. Our Gun Boats has not done any thing yet only to take Torpedoes out of the Channel. Two of our Monitors and One Musgueto Boat was sunk by those adomable things One was a Two Terited Moniter and sunk on a sand bar and broke in two   the other one probably will be raised. We belong to the First Brigade 2nd Division 13th A C The A C is commanded by Gen Granger Our Division by Gen Andrews the 2nd Divis is with Steel with the Exception of our Brig Well Jane I have not had a letter from you since we left the Cove the 17th of March. This part of Alabama is very broken and a very poor country. We are in sight of Mobile We can see the Rebles Boats a runing around Well Jane probably this will be the last letter that I will write untill the place is taken, so you need not expect many letters from me for a while. I must close for this time from your affectionate Husband S. I. Shearer to E. J. Shearer

Parts of a letter

you have any let me know whether you have enough to do you untill my time is out. If I knew that you had money to do you I believe that I would not draw any before that time We may not get any money before that time and we may get pay soon. Our Brigade Commander says that we will be paid before we leave this place. Well I must tell you where we are at the present time, yesterday morning we marched to this place. It is about five miles from our oald camp, we are now camped in the Woods among the Swamps. The land here is all sand where there is know water, and I presume it is the same under the water, in this part of the Country is very many swamps. There is a strip of dry land about four or five rods wide and veries in length, and then a swamp about the same width, this is the way the land is here from the Gulf to the Bay, it is Timbered with Pitch Pine It is a very poor country in my estimation. I understand that there is about a Brigade of Rebles about Twenty miles from this place I presume that they are there a watching our movements. I donot anticipate much hard fighting in this part of the country unless the Rebles get a great deal of reinforcement. Our Army will be large enough to whip all the Rebles combined in Alabama. It will probably be three or four weeks before we have much marching to do. It is rumored that our Brigade has the preference of being Station at Mobile after it is Capture untill our time is out the Regt in this Brigade all go out about the same time. Well I would like to see Mobile it is said to be such a nice place and I would as soon stay there as any other place that I know of, but it is not our luck to get to stop at any place like that Well Jane I presume that our Colonel will ware a Star before long or at least I have been informed so, and I have heard it said that he was just a Private. I hear that he is to be sent to some other Brigade and that he is a trying to get the 23rd out of this Brigade in to the one that he is to Command. I wish he would let us alone we can get along without him, he has us changed from one Brig to an other once about every two months and he has not bettered our conditions yet, he came very night geting us in that Red River Scrape that Banks had last Spring he got Started a little to late was all that Saved us. I believe that he would Sacrifice the last man for the Sake of geting him a Star. Well Jane the maile is to go out today at Twelve OClock and I hardly know what to fill my letters up with. Well I will say this I have made five vests since we came to Ala. I made one for myself and If I live I expect to take it home with me. I got one dollar and half a piece for making them when I had nothing else to do I could make a vest in a day. I could have made several other vests, but it is hard workin these dog tents. Well Jane it has been cloudy and rainey weather pretty nigh every since we have been in Ala. Well Jane I must close for this time, hopeing to get a letter soon anouncing the health of you and the children no more at present from your affectionate Husband S. I Shearer to E. J. Shearer.

When this you see remember me

Spanish Landing Alabama
April the 18th 1865

Dear Wife I take the present opportunity to write you a fiew lines to let you know that I am well and hearty at present and I hope that these fiew lines may find all of you well and hearty. I received three letters from you, the 8th Inst and one from Jake Crouch. I was very much pleased to hear from you that you ware all well at present. I was glad to hear that my things has got threw, they are worth considerable to me if I get home. Well Jane you said that you pap would like to have a Cavalry Over Coat if I can get one for him I will do it but it is a geting to late in the season I expect it will almost impossible to get one now I could have got all the coats that I wanted when we started on this campane but I had know way of taking care of them or sending them home therefore I would not bother with them. I would like very much to have one of theme myself but I expect I cannot get one. Well Jane I wrote you a letter the 8th Inst. I said then probably it would be the last one untill the fall of Mobile. We captured these forts at 10 AM of the

9th I dont know the exact amount of prisoners that was taken. The Forts ware evacuated but fiew of the Rebs got away As soon as this place was taken our Brig was left to guard the Prisoners and Forts and the balance of the Troops went to Blakely and in a day or two they captured that they got nigh Three Thousand Prisoners at that place and they ware sent down for us to guard and yesterday the Stars and Stripes could be seen floating over Mobile. Mobile was surrendered with Two Thousand State Militia. Two Regt that we are or that the Remainder of our Regt is guarding is all boys. A portion of them are very small for Soldiers. From what I can learn we have captured about Twenty Thousand Prisoners including those that Gen Thorn has captured besides the killed and wounded This campaine is one of the most successful campains that I ever seen Our Regt is divided a part of them is at the Fort guarding Prisoners and the Balance of us is at the Landing for fatigue and Picket duty. I would not be surprised if we went back to the Miss without seeing Mobile. Tell Matilda I am glad that some of my oald friends has not forgotten me The mail is going out and I must close My respects to all Enquireing Friends Your affection Husband Silas Shearer to E. J. Shearer

Blakely Alabama
May the 5th 1865

Dear Wife I take the present Opportunity to write you a fiew lines to inform you that I am well and hearty. I am lame in my right arm it was caused by throwing a Shell. I was marked off of duty Two days on the account of it. My arm is getting better. This was the first time that I have been off of duty for nigh Two Years. I hope that these fiew lines may find all you well and hearty and Enjoying pleasure. Well Jane it has been sometime since I have had a letter from you and I would like to hear from home again but I must not complain if I cannot get a letter Every week because I have not writen to you as I should have done, but I can excuse myself very Easy and I think that you will look over it, the reason that I have not writen more frequent was because I was scarce of paper and I did not know how soon I could get any paper and I thought that I would keep my paper to answer you letters but I have got money at last and I can write to you when ever I feel like so doing. We was paid for the Ten Months the other day Well the money looked very nice to me. It has been one year save three days since we got any pay. I have not sent any money yet and I donot know when I will The rumor is now that we will go to New Orleans soon. If that is the case I will keep my money untill I get there. It will not cost me as much and then not the danger of Torpedoes. If we donot go to New Orleans soon I will try and go to Mobile and Express it from there. We are within Eight miles of Mobile and I have not been there yet   some of the boys has been over and they say it is a very nice place.

Jeannie how would you like to live in Mobile. I think I would like the place very well. Mobile gives a discharged Soldier a good chance for to get a start in the World it lies on the Bay where the Sea Breeze is all the time in motion and plenty of Oysters all the time and I presume fish are plenty Also we have a breeze all the time here, but know Town, and not a very nice place, and I guess it is very unhealthy. I presume that we will leave this part of the Country before the sicly season comes The weather is tolerable warm at this time. I received a letter from Mother the other night They ware geting along very well but she knowes nothing of my Brothers. I fear they was on that Boat that was destroid and losing so many lives The Paper said that they ware Andersonvill Prisoners on there way home. A many a brave man lost his live by carlesness and probably intentionly done. Well Jane we have just got order to move at an early hour in the morning I understand that it is to Mobile if so I will close untill we get there Good by my Dear Sat 6th we probably will not move from here today, if we go to Mobile Transportation has not come yet. Well Jane when I heard of the death of Lincoln it appeared to me that I had lost one of my mighest Friends. He was the Soldiers best Friend, but he had done Enough in this World and the kind hand of providence called him home to live in peace. Well Jennie I have seen a great many Rebles Soldiers. Here they take the Oath and go home I have seen some of Lees men a going threw here and they are very glad to get home. They say they will not fight the Yankees again but they will fight the bushwackers. There is a Company of State Militia Organizing here and some Reble Soldiers belong to it, they are going to protect the Country. Well Jane I was apointed Treasurer of the Iowa Soldiers Orphan Asylum for Co K our Company did not go in to it very deep but the last account our Regt was a head. Our Regt is made up of as honest and as splended set of men as I Ever seen They are in for helping the Soldiers Orphan all they can. I hope that they will be rewarded for it. Well Jane you have sent me a great many stamps and now I will send you a little present in five and ten cent pieces of new paper money You needent send me any more Stamps untill I send for them I must close Your Affection Husband Silas I Shearer to Elizabeth J. Shearer

Camp 23" Iowa Near Mobile, Ala
May the 12th 1865

Dear Wife I seat myself to pen you a fiew lines to let you know that I am well and hearty at present and I sincerly hope that these fiew lines may find all of you well and hearty and Enjoying pleasure. I received your letter today dated the 27th of April it was read with pleasure. nothing pleases me better than to hear that you are all well but I am sorrow to think that you are uneasy about me for I have got threw safe thus far and I presume that you are informed of it before this You have heard of the capture of Mobile and the Casualities of the Regt Engagaed I have written to you about it before this and probably you have got the letters. I hope so at any rate so as you will know that I am not hurt by the Rebs at this place, and from all accounts there will not be very much danger anymore on this side at least. I have faith to believe it, you think that the assassination of Lincoln has maid dark hours in the North. Well I presume that it did. It looked dark in the South and a great deal darker to the Rebs because they think that there best friend was killed, but Johnson has followed his footsteps with the Exception of more stringent orders and that is what the Soldiers want to hear and the Rebles leaders think there necks are in more danger in Johnson hands than if Lincoln had lived, but since that time how things have changed Darkeness has very nigh gon and I can see day light aproaching. I think that the fighting is over at any rate on this side and our glorious Country will again be United with stronger feeling than ever. Well Jane I went to Mobile today and Expressed some money it is expressed in Fathers name to Nevada Now I will give the list of money Expressed. I sent One Hundred (130) Thirty Dollars, Dave Perlin One Hundred (145) Dollars, Henry I Perin One Hundred (125) Dollars all of it amounting to Four Hundred Dollars. Now Jane I must tell you how this money matter stands. I and the Express Agent made a mistake of One Hundred (100) Dollars We counted the Money and only made Three Hundred (300) of it and there was Four Hundred (400) Dollars put in the package and only Three Hundred (300) Dollars of it Insured. The Insurance is only paid on Three Hundred (300) of it and the other is going threw unpaid if it goes at all. If you get the package and it is not opened you will get One Hundred (100)Dollars with out paying the Insurance on it and if it is opened at Nevada and the Four Hundred (400) Dollars is in it pay the Freight on the unpaid money. If there is but Three Hundred (300) Dollars gets threw Pay Dave and Henry there amount and you will have Thirty (30) Dollars left. Give One Hundred (145) to Daves wife and One Hundred (125) Dollars to Mrs. McDowell for Henry Perin. I got a joke on the Express Agent but if he gets the Hundred (100) Dollars the Joke is turned Well Jane that is rather a joke on Bob Heath but if we will hold on he will get threw without paying any money and will have to do know fighting I understand that all Recruits and Drafted men that have not joined There Regt will be Discharged ammediatly if I am not on duty tomorrow I will write some more I will close for this evening Your Husband Silas I Shearer to E. J. Shearer

Misc parts of letters

Well Jane from what you Said that Hintz has been playing Hot with the girls. I expect they did not feel as well at the end of Nine Months as they did at the begining of the Same but they will have to put up with it Well I expect Mary Thompson got a very bad wound from Bill but I guess that the Bayonet thrust did not hurt her very much but it seemes to be a kind of poison that Stays in the wound which growes worse and worse for Seveal months. I expect She is glad of it I think she wanted to be wounded in such a manner I am like you are I do not want any more increase untill I am home to stay and therefore I expect I had better not come home on a furlough by the time I would get home I would not have no more Sence than to start one I expect you would rather I would not come home on a furloug if I would do such a trick as that to start an increase in the family but let that be as it may I would like to See you and to Sleep with you once again and to kiss those sweet lips that I like so well How the past flies threw my memory I think of the pleasures we once enjoyed I want you to let me know what Jake has done to Kit in the Secret line Keep this to youself from you loveing Husband Silas I. Shearer to E. J. Shearer

Well Jane I will write a fiew lines on this peace of paper We had a nice Shower of rain yesterday and last night and the air is fresh and reviveing today and signes of more rain I am on Camp guard today I was first on this morning and I was on duty Six hours and then a Sergeant of Co H tendes to the guards. Six hours I will come on again fifteen minutes after Nine Oclock to night and will be on untill fifteen minutes of Three in the morning then my time will be up for at present and I am in hopes that I will not come on duty again while in the Service. I will tell you who is on guard today from our Co. Corporal Steward Bill Thompson, Town, Ross Wilson, and myself and I have the worst time on the account of being up so long at a time. Well Jane I never have writen to you what I was you see by that Co record that I was a Corporal that list was maid last Sumer while at Morganza I presume I am a Sergeant for that is what they call me and I am detailed as such. I must close from your affectionate Husband S. I. Shearer to E. J. Shearer

Well Jane a suprise drill is to go off next Thursday the 7th in our Corps it is done in this way One Company of Each Regt in Each Brigade drills against Each other and the Company that wins the prise in the Brigade goes to the Division and the prise Company of the Several Brigades drill together and the prise Company of each Division goes to the Corps and the Company that is the best gets the large prise. Company H of our Regt is to drill for the prise they will be some Scientific drilling done the majority of this Corp is very well drilled. Some troops left here last night It is said they went down the River No one except the Commanders knowes where they went to Probably they went to drive some gurilles from the river. Well we have a new Regt in our Brigade it is the 35th Wisconsin they havent been out but a short time If we acted as green when we first came out as they do I do not wonder at other Boys laughin at us They have Seven or Eight Women with them and they belong to the privates and Non Commission. I cannot see what use they have for Women in the Army It is not a decent place for them. Soldiers in the field gets very hard and it maters but little to them what they do and Say and if the fair Sex does not want to See and hear them they will have to Shut there eyes and Stop there Ears. A great many that follows the Army would not Shut there Eyes nor Stop there Ears but if they want to Stay with the Army I have no objection I am sure.

S.I.S. to E. J. S.

Parts of Others

Well Jane this is the 13th and it is very Cold for the last two nights, and then gets very Warm threw the day Such weather I think is very unhealthy. Although the health of the Regt is good at this time. Well Jane the two last Reble Gunboats Surrendered to Commodore Thatcher at 3:45 p.m. on Thursday last The Two Boats and Crew have came down to Mobile. A great many Reble Transports has come to Mobile in the last fiew days. Reb Soldiers is comin all the time. There is as many Reb Soldiers in Mobile as ther is of our own and they seem to be satisfied The majority of them thinks that the war is over. They are willing to Stop Fighting and go home and try and be Citizens of the United States once more. Well Jane I heard yesterday that the cars run Five Hundred miles on the Mobile and the Ohio Railroad I donot know how true it is but it will not be long untill the Rail Road will be repaired so the Cars can run threw. The State of Ala will be reorganized before many months rolls around the Citizens are apealing to the Legislature to Convene and make some efforts to be restored to the Union They seem to be very ancious to be Governed by the Laws of the Government but they Say that Slavery is no more. I am of the same Opinion. I think Slavery is Dead and I am thankful for it I always thaught that Slavery was rong but I was Opposed to Meddling with it as long as the United States was in Peace but after the South began fighting us and would except of know terms but there Independance then I wanted to see Slavery wiped out and I thank fortune it has been done and I think we will have a free Government Once again. Well Jane I will close for this time from you Effectionate Husband Silas I. Shearer to Elizabeth J. Shearer

Camp four miles South of Mobile
May 8, 1865

Dear Wife I seat myself to write you a fiew lines to let you know that I am well and hearty at present and enjoying Soldiers life the best I can I sincerely hope that these fiew lines may find all of you well and hearty and enjoying pleasure. Well Jane I received a letter from you yesterday it bear date April the 12th I was glad to hear from you again To hear that you was well and hearty. Well Jennies we moved from Blakely the Evening of the 7th. It was dark when we marched threw Mobile. We did not get to see but little of the City. We marched four miles South of the City We got threw by nine Oclock P.M. It began to rain soon after we left the City and continued untill after we got threw. We have a very nice place for a Camp. The 20th Wis Vols was the first Regt that came to this camp, the 84th Ill was the next Regt and then the 23rd Iowa. These three Regt is all that is in this Camp with the Exception of a Battery, the 18th Iowa belonged to our Brigade, but they have gone to Fort Gaines. One month ago these three Regt would have had fun to lay here. The Rebles would have quarrell considerable about the ground, but now we lay here unmolested. We have know Pickets out to keep the Rebles off of us. The Coln Com'd the Brigade says all that we have to do is to keep clean and to do the necessary guard and fatigue that is required for Camp. He sayes that we will not remain here more than Ten Days or Two weeks and then we will go to New Orleans. What we will do then I cannot tell. Well as we was marching threw the City a little girl wanted to know whether we was coming home. I was up to the City yesterday and I stoped in a grocery and the woman that was in wanted to know whether we was a going to be discharged here and I could not tell her. Well Jane I seen some pretty and nice ladies here in Mobile and there is considerable many of them. They are the Sociablest Set of Citizens that I have seen in any part of the South. They ware all supprised to see our men conduct themselves so well. They say that our men appear more like Gentlemen than the Confederate Soldiers did they praise our Soldiers for there behaveior Some of the big Southern men say that our men behaves them selves a great deal better than they supposed from what they heard. Our Camp is on the Bay and we get the Sea Breeze all the time and that is the healthiest breeze that blowes. Well Jennie I understand that Order is now for those Troops that has Clothing and Commissaries to last them untill the first of June is not alowed to draw any more clothing. Coln Glasgow says that he is a going to try get us a Suit a piece about the time we get ready to go home. Whether he can do it is more than I can say. Some think we will go out of the service soon. Well every thing bids fair for it at present but things may take a change in a short time. We have nothing to do on this side The Rebles are done fighting they are tired of fighting We may have to go on the other side of the River to fight the Rebles down, but they are fools if they keep on and draw an Army over there It will ruin their Country if our Government has got to send a Army in there They will devastate the Country as they go. They will have know mercy on them for our men thinks they are whiped according to the rules of War, and they will not let them much more. Well Jane this is the pretiest part of the South that I have seen. I have seen nice green peas for sale in the City, this is Early then you can raise in the North Well Jane if it was not for you and the dear Children I would go to Mexico instead of going home but I must go home to my dear little family, which I so much loved. When I am discharged you can expect me home if I live and I will not be any longer on the road than posible the shorter the time I have to stay the more I want to see you but that is a natural consequence. I must close for this time your affectionate Husband Silas I Shearer to E.J.S.

We parted with a cheerful smile,
When last I pressed here hand,
To follow to the battle-field
The Banner of our land.
Her glowing glance in memory
Uncessingly will burn,
For well I know she will bestow
The same when I return.

When gazing at the glimmering stars,
And resting on the ground,
While soldiers, wearied by the March,
Are slumbering around,
How oft, to hold that little hand,
And hear her vows I yearn,
For well I know she will bestow
The Same when I return.

-S. I. Shearer

Well Jane I am writing by Candle Light We have had a nice Shower of rain this Evening and good prospect for more rain to night. Well we have to march at 6 1/2 Oclock in the Morning I understand that we will go aboard the Alis Vivian and cross the bar and then reship on the Gen Sedgwich, bound for Galveston I presume if I get threw Safe I shall write to you as soon as possible. Well Jane I was talking to Dave about that money and he is willing to loose his part of that money. The amount would be thirty three and one third Dollars a piece I told them that

Thirty Three Dollars a peace would be all that I would ask of them and I would loose Thirty Four Dollars Father can count it up for himself and then he will know that he is right Henry Perins Ninety Two ($92) Dollars Dave Perin One Hundred and Twelve ($112) dollars and myne is Ninety Six ($96) Dollars they have given there consent to this. I presume that there Signature not needed that will do for the money.

Well Jane I am a going to Espress a box of Clothing in the Morning if I can   if it is expressed it will be expressed in Fathers name to Nevada. You will find an over coat in it and if Father wants an Over Coat he can have his choice of this coat and the one that is at home. If I express the Clothing I will write some more in here with a pencil this Clothing is for myself. Well Jane I presume that we will not get out of the Service untill the Experation of our term of Elistment and we have three months from today to serve if we have to stay in. I must close hopeing to see you soon
Your affectionate Husband S. I. Shearer to E. J. Shearer
This Box of Clothing is Expressed to Nevada

Camp 23rd Iowa Near Mobile Ala
May 21st 1865

Dear Wife I seat myself this morning to write you a fiew lines to let you know that I am well and hearty at present and I hope that these fiew lines may find all of you well and hearty Well Jane I received a letter from you Friday Evening the 19th Inst I was glad to hear from you again and to hear that you was right side up with care I am in hopes that Father and Mother is well and hearty again Well Jane if nothing hapens more than what is anticipated we will not get very many more letters down here I have understood that our maile is a going to be detained at Cairo if such is the case all the maile that we will get is maile that is below that place Well Jane we are here in our oald camp high Mobile how much longer we will stay here I cannot tell. The 20th Wis Regt belonging to our Brigade has got the mustering out papers. I understand that they are to be discharged the Second day of June Our officers has orders to Square up there books ready for mustering out I understand that we are to be a Mustered out the 15th of June. The Coln says we will be mustered out in Three Weeks as soon as the books is maid out we will start for Iowa. There is to be a Grand Review of the Troops here in a fiew days then something will be done. Troops that is to be Mustered Out will be started to there respected places of Musterout and those that are to be retained in the field will be reorganized. I understand that the recruits is to be taken out of the Regt that is to go out and transfered to Regt that is to be kept in the service. Well Jane I write a great deal of this from flying reports I know this much, that the Officers had Orders and have been at work at the books to have them ready for Musteringout. Our time is not very long if we have to serve it out. You needent look for me untill you see me comeing and then you can look for things are uncertain in the Army. From what I can see and learn I think we will be at home by the Fourth of July or on the road at least. The shorter the time we have to serve the longer it seems to be. Every day that rolls around makes me want to see you more and more I long to see the time when we will get home so we can have some more pleasure Well Jane I am glad that you have got that clothing that I sent with Dave. Well Jane you wrote in a letter some time ago that Jerry Stall was not a maried man but he would be when he got home. If going in to the Service makes a man Single I should have put myself to some of the Southern Aristocricy long ago for Stall is a Maried man and a Father of Nine Children or at least he sayes he hase to Daddy them Well Jane I have to gass a little alook over it A man can get a wife in this part of the Country for any length of time that he wants He can get her for lifetime one night or for a fiew minutes just as he likes but such I do not like Well I must close hoping I will see you soon so no more at present your Affectionate Husband Silas I Shearer to Elizabeth J. Shearer

PS Well Jane I and Dave and Henry Perin sent some money to Nevada in Fathers name it is as follows Dave $145 One Hundred and Forty Five Dollars Henry $125 Dollars and I sent $130 Dollars makeing four hundred dollars in all but by mistake only $300 Dollars was insured if there is only $300 Dollars gets threw give Daves to Martha and Henrys to McDowell and there will be $30 dollars left for me if $400 gets threw I will have $130 Dollars I will send the receipt in this letter.

Parts of other letters

Well Jane I have been trying to tell you something about the Ft but I cannot with the pen. I can tell you more about it if I get home. I must put these in for life is very uncertain and we may get among the blew pills that the Rebls has and that is very unholsum to a great many of us. Well Jane I have not seen Ft. Gaines we passed Ft Powel it was a Fort situated in the water at a point of land. it commanded one pass. This pass is called Grants pass. This pass is just wide enough for Boats to pass. The Rebles filled the channel with obstruction so as it would be dangerous for our Boats to Pass. Fort Morgan commands the other pass But our Boats run apass the Fort (you are aware of that) and captured the Ram Tenn" Admiral Fariget said that if he has been on the Tennessee he could have whiped the whole fleet. Well Jane we heard a lecture from a Mr. Engles on the question of the Orphan Asylum. He is a Methodist preacher and he speaks very well on the subject. He gives a very clear idea of things. He will get considerable of Money in our Regt as in all Iowa Regt that he has seen. The Resilutions of our Company will be published in a Marshalltown Paper. A great many of the boys in our Co is very Stingy and they thought it would do there Children no good and they would not apropraite one Cent, but they would spend other wise and benefit know one but the one that got the money. Well Jane I will have to appeal to you for Stamps if you want to hear from me, if not, you can keep the Stamps, but I expect I will see some Stamps, one or two Stamps at a time will be sufficient at present. I have got two from you here lately. I have know money to buy with and If I had I could not get them at present. Jane I sent you a song ballad headed the *Wife of the Volunteer* if you got it I want you to let me know it. Well Jane you had better not write anything to me that you would not like any one else to know for I cannot tell where I will be in a month from now from you affectionate Husband Silas I. Shearer to E. J. Shearer This man that lectured last night is from Iowa I would love to see all of you my Dear

Ballad sent home
"Wife of the Volunteer"

Yes, Jane, I have come, love, across the dark blue sea,
To our peaceful, quiet home, love, our little ones and thee;
I've watch'd and waited nightly for the Welcome hour to come,
When hapily and frightly all the dear delights of home
Should greet my listening Ear, love, upon my native shore;
Then wipe away thy tears, Jane, for I will roam no more.

How often since I left you, love, in solitude and tears,
Have I bless'd that love which clung to me threw many changing years;
And while I paced the silent beat, forgotten and alone,
Has my heart recall'd they love-lit smile, thy
sweet and gentle tone.
Thy image, love, has ever been shrined within this fond hearts core;
But wipe away thy tears, love, for I will roam no more.

Dear Jane, when in life's sweet morn, in all thy youthful pride,
I love thee, Virgin, bathed in tears from thy fond mother's side,
And I promised at the Altar to love through life as now,
Say, Jane, when life's sorrow came, did I forget that Vow?
Your heart will own I left you, love, our Country to Restore;
Then wipe away thy tears, love, for I will rome no more.

-by S. I. Shearer

Camp 23" Iowa Near Mobile Ala
May 26th 1865

Dear Wife I take the present opportunity to write you a fiew lines to let you know that I am well and hearty at present and enjoying myself the best I can. I hope these fiew lines will find all of you well and hearty. Well Jane we are not gon from Mobile yet We are still in our oald Camp and not knowing how long we will remain here Probably not long very likely we will leave this place between this and the fifth of June. General Andrews reviewed us the other day and he said that we would be reviewed once more before we go home. I understand that the Review is to take place on Oald Gen Jackson Battleground at New Orleans. I presume that this is flying reports for I have not seen it in the papers and if it was

148

that would not confirm it unless the Commanding General name was at the bottom of the piece This review so say reports is to take place on the 10th of June if this takes place as soon as it is over we will go home I presume Well Jane time rolls off very slow to me at this time We are about four miles South of Mobile it is a very nice Camp but very lonesome to me. We are on the Shell road and there is a great deal of travel on the road but it does not interest me I see a great many of the Soldiers a pleasure riding with the ladies of Mobile I am glad to see Soldiers Enjoy themselves If we had know hopes of geting home untill our time was out time would not seem so long to me We are Expecting Orders Everyday to go to New Orleans When a Soldier is waiting and Expecting Orders then time goes slow to them The Officers are makeing out the Musteringout Rolls today are geting very nigh threw with the Copy Roll for all that it may be Sometime before we are musteredout and it may be but a Short time. I have come to the conclusion that if this letter does not reach you until the 12" or 15" of June you stop writing untill further orders. I presume if nothing hapens that we will be on our road home by that time if such is the case I would not get you letters that is writen after you get this. I presume that you know as much about these things as I do probably a good deal more. Our Brig" is all prepareing to be Mustered out, the 20th Wis" have there Rolls printed ready for Mustering out they are now awaiting the Descision whether they shall be Musteredout at New Orleans or go to the State. The Coln" that Comdg" our Brigd" is the Coln" of the 20" Wis Regt and he is trying to get us Mustered Out at New Orleans. Whether he will succeed or not I can not tell but I hope so I would like to go up the River a Citizen. However look for me when you see me a comeing then you will not have to look very long Well Jane yesterday a little after 2 OClock in the afternoon one of the most sad accidents hapened in Mobile since the War began. The Explosion of Amunition that was stored in a cotton press in the upper part of the City. There was about Two Hundred Ton of Amunition a large quantity of powder and a great deal of fixed Shell for large Cannon. Fixed Shell is Shell that is filled and primed ready for use. The Amunition was being removed Axidently a Soldier droped a percusion Shell and it Exploded and set fire to the powder and it Exploded destroying about half of the City and three or four boats. Eight Blooks ware all destroyed tareing down buildings hardly leaving one brick upon an other and Seting fire to a great many buildings About Eight Square making 32 Blooks was more or less injured the Transport Coln Cowles was set a fire and burned up.

The Cate Dale was blowen to pieces by the Concussion of the Air and two more Boats destroid that I cannot name. Up to this morning about Two Hundred persons dead and Wounded have been taken out from the buildings and rublish that lays threw the City no one can tell how many more will be found A great many of our Soldiers was quartered in Cotton Presses nigh the place where the Explosion took place and the buildings was throwen down on them and killed and wounded the Majority of them People that has seen the destruction say it is the horriblest sight that they Ever Seen men women and Children was hurt Some with there legs and arms Broken and Some with there legs and arms torn off Men was killed a mile from where the Explosion took place Men ware killed and not a Scratch to be see on there person The Concussion of the Aire was what done the damage to the City I never heard such a report before in my life. Shells are Exploding yet this morning. It supposed that about Two or Three Thousand Soules have been hurt the loss in the City is Estimated at Ten Million ($10,000,000) of Dollars This was about one third of the Amunition Surrendered by Gen" Dick Taylor It mashed a train of cars that was Standing ready to go out Considerable of the property destroid was Government Property Well Jane this is the morning of the 27th The reason I did not finish my letter yesterday was that Downs and I went to the City to see the Destruction I never seen a Town so badly injured in my life it is wors than any place that we have Sieged. There was not many White Soldiers hurt. Know Regt of White Soldiers was Covered up in the ruins as was the first report. The Two Co of Negroes that was at work with the amunition was all destroid. Downs and I went as nigh the place were the amunition was before Exploding as we could for the Smoke Shells ware Still bursting and continue to burst this morming. While we was in there we Seen a human of some kind His lower Extremities was all gon as high as the upper part of his hips Both Armes gone to the Elbow his Head was all gone but one Eare. I presume probably that it was a negro he was badly burned the first sight a person could not tell what it was. Cotton was sticken to the Skin which give it the appearance of a part of a Sheep By close Examination we could see that it had been a human of some kind. I was talking to one the Sentinels that was nigh when the Explosion took place He said that a Shell Exploded about Two Seconds before the great Explosion took place From what he said it lookes reasonable that Some one droped a Pecussion Shell and it Exploded Siting the remainder of the power on Fire. A great deal of Cotton was destroid also but the fire Engines are at work trying to quench the fire as fast as possible. I seen a woman that was very uneasy She was watching the Cotton Especialy the Cotton that was in one buliding From what I could learn the Cotton belonged to her A great deal of the Cotton belonged to individuals and it was all the way that they had of making any thing at present. Well Jane this is the Eighth and my letter not finished yet but I will try and finish it today. I went on Brig Guard yesterday morning in the place of John Steward he wanting to go to the City I was relieved this moring therefore I did not get to finish the letter Well Jane I drank a quart of Buttermilk this morning at Breakfast It cost me Ten Cents and I thought it was Excellent and I have had all the blackberrys that I could eat several times but they are not as good here as they are North Well Jane yesterday Evening a Circular came to the Brig Head Quarters from General Granger anouncing the Surrender of Kirby Smith I presume it is so Some thinks we will not get home so soon by his Surrendering as we would if he had not I think we will get home just as soon Concerning your writing letters you can do as you please. I presume that you know as much about it as I do Well Jane I will close hopeing that I will see you soon no more at present Your Affectionate Husband S I Shearer to E. J. Shearer

Camp 23 Iowa Near Mobile Ala
June 1" 1865

Dear Wife I take the present opportunity to write you a fiew lines to let you know that I am well and hearty at present and I hope that these fiew lines may find all of you well and hearty. I received a letter from you the 29" of May it bear date May the 8th. I was well pleased to heare from you again Well Jane I wish I could have been at home to help or taken you place while planting corn before this Well Jane I am Sorrow to hear that the papers publishes so much false news about us geting home. I presume that you have us Musteredout at home that is what I can learn from Every one that gets letters from home and here we are not musteredout yet and know definet Orders as to Musteringout Troops in this Department. No Orders only to make out the books and to Square up the papers preparitory to Musteringout. I presume that Orders will be here soon to Musterout Troops but I cannot tell what Troops that will be I presume that you are looking for me Every minute but still I donot come. Well Jane by the 10" or 15" of this month we will be sent to Galveston or Brownsville Texas Now I expect this is surprising to you but this is so if the Orders is not changed I understand that it is a voluntary act in the Commanders of the Regt Six Thousand is called for in the 13" Ala to go to Texas and the Regt that will volunteer and go has the preference and Coln Glasgow like he always done has got 23rd Regt to go. He is always trying to get this Regt to go where they donot want to go and where he has know business He has got the men and Officers down on him by so doing the Officers has given him to understand what they think of him and he has learned that the men are all down on him. The Officers and men of the Regt know that the Rebelion is crushed and peace has come to our Country again and now they are ancious to get home where they can Enjoy some pleasure again. I presume that Coln Glasgow makes a great deal more money here in the Army than he can at home and probably lives as well and an other thing that makes him want to go to Texas he wants to get as many of the 23" as he can to go with him to Mexico and he thinks the higher he gets the better it is the more men he will get to go with him. Now I cannot see it in that light A great many of the boys wants to go to Mexico but if he is acting in this way he would get but fiew to go with him I would like to go to Mexico myself but if it is the Coln fault that we go to Texas I would not go with him to Mexico if I had but Three Rods to go to get a cross the line If I went from Texas I would go on my

151

own hook if it was'ent that you have been at your paps so long I would go to Mexico from Texas if we go there. Well Jane I wrote to you in my other letter that it would be useless for you to write any more after geting it but the prospects of getting home is prolonged probably we will have to serve our time out and a Month or two in adition to our time. I am Shure that I can stand it if I donot get sick but I would like to get home before the 18th of September so as I could prepare for Winter. The majority of the boys in this Regt are Farmers and they would like to get home Well Jane I am Sorrow to hear that Jacob Crouch is dissatisfied with his new Country If he gets back to Marshall Co he will not be Satisfied but a short time Well Jane it is very pleasant writing this morning in the Shade but I will close for this time and we will see where I am when I write again your affectionate Husband Silas I. Shearer to E. J. Shearer

Camp 23" Iowa Mobile Ala
June 15, 1865

Dear Wife Youres of the 1" Inst arived yesterday it was received and read with pleasure as all letters are that comes from home I am well and hearty at present and I hope that these fiew lines may find all of you well and hearty. Well Jane I received a letter from you five or six days ago and did not answer it. We thought awhile that we was agoing to go home and then we got orders to be ready to go aboard of a Sea going vessel and I presume that our distination was Galveston Therefore I thought I would not write untill we got to our Journeys end but the order has been Countermended and I cannot tell what we will do General Sheridan will be here in a day or two I presume that we can tell what we will do I think we will be started home soon after he reviews us. If it was not for crossing the water I would like to go to Galveston I hardly think now that we will go to Galveston Although I may be fooled in it. We are lying in our oald Camp and the boys are geting very tired of it but I still live in hopes they say they have done all that they have come out to do and now they want to go home and I do not blame them. Well Jane I am glad to hear that the prospects for Crops are tolerable good I would like to see abundance of produce this Fall I am ancious to get another letter from you to know whether that money got threw safe or not If it gets home safe I will be satisfied if the next letter comes threw as quick as the last one did it will not be long untill I will hear from the Money I think when you get the money that you will not delay an hour in writing to me concerning it for One Hundred Dollars is considerable to loose it one pull I think that the money is all right I hope so anyway. I am glad to hear that Elias has got to St. Louis I presume acording to the order that he will be Discharged soon and now I would like to hear from Andrew probably he is at some place where he has better care taken of him or some place where he can get plenty to ware and to eat. I presume that the boys seen hard times while they ware prisoners. I am in hopes that they will boath get home soon to enjoy some pleasure again Well Jane you said that Denna was a going to school I am glad that he likes to go to School and I see that you are anxious for him to go to School That is one good idea in youre head. I want the Children to have good Education and I am glad that you are of the same notion I want my Children to have good Education if they get nothing else I always thought that you was a good Mother to Children and the more I know of you the more I am convinced of the fact I do not want you to force him to go to School yet for he is to young if he wants to go all right if you could have your way youse would have a preacher of him before he was 12 years old I have been listening to hear of Elle a going to School Denna is like his pap he thinks if he can get to go to school he will get rid of work a very good Idea. Heh! Well Jane you have never said what you have done with that place of ourn Whether the ground is Idle or not. I have sometimes thought the way that you write that it is planted to Corn. I am in hopes that such is the Case and that the Crops will be good I understand that the bugs and worms is Injuring the Wheat potatoes and Even the plumbs in some parts of the State. Well Jane you said sometime ago that Pap wanted a Cavalry Coat but it was to late The Cavalry Coats ware all sold that could be had at a reasonable price. I bought an Inft Overcoat it is a very large Inftry Coat it cost me five dollars and he can have one or the other of the Coats as I cannot get an other one. If I do not get home in time I want you to get some Hay cut if you can. S I Shearer

Camp 23" Iowa Near Mobile Ala
June 18 1865

Dear Wife Youres of the 4" Inst arived today. I am well and hearty at present and I hope that these fiew lines may find all of you well and hearty and Enjoying greater Sadisfaction than you did when your letter was writen Well Jane you wrote that you got that package of Money that I sent and you say that Three Hundred Dollars was the amount that was received Well that was rather a hard blow but it cant be helped now Well you say what went with the other you cannot tell if I put it in the Envelope. I write to you what become of the money if it did not get threw I have proof for this Henry P. Perin is the man. You write as though you think it is doubtful whether I sent the money or not Will it seemes as though Gambling is on the minds of a great many people and you donot know whether I gamble or not if you would ask that question I could tell you. You know that Jane. Your are right if I gamble I am different from the time I last saw you but War changes a great many things and probably has changed me All things will come to light. You seem to feel very bad about it you take trouble to Easy it is useless to Cry about anything that is passed I presume that you will not be on the County yet for a while You generaly flinch before you are pricked if loosing that Hundred Dollars brings you on the County times certainly are very dark in Iowa A great deal more than they are here. I presume that you will hardly miss that money and you will not have to work any harder than then you did heretofore. Well you want to know how I made such a mistake in Counting Money and If I did make such a mistake. I am to be pitied probably you think I was drunk crazy or did not know very much One thing I will admit and the other you will have to guess at I admit that I know very little but yet I knows enough to Eat when I get Hungry. Yes I admit that if I spent that Money a gambling or in any other way and then write to you that I sent the Money to you it would be rather a shame on me to think that I spent money and did not want you to know how I spent it or what it was for Probably you may think that I spent it in some of these Houses in Mobile I guess hardly you want to know why Dave & Henry will not Stand there share of the loss how do you know but what they will. Henry says he will loose his part. Dave has not said anything about it yet but to go in to the masures that you propose is very hard work and pore pay It is work that I never fancied and I hardly think that I will take the job You say that Dave sends more money home than any other one that you know of He sent her a present of Ten Dollars and sent One Hundred and Forty Five Dollars You think that he does not spend any money or does something that he is very lucky in. Well Dave is so Stingy that he hardly goes to do his business he would hardly spend if he was with his wife. Well Martha has room to feel large over her Husband It is but fiew that sends all of there Money home and you seem to feel very bad because she gets more money then you do but still you do not care if I spend it in an honest way What do you call dishonest Well you know that we was not paid for Ten Months and my Tobacco bill was about Twenty Dollars. While Dave was a punishing himself to save a little but he has gone to Smoking and Chewing again. When we was paid I was in debt to the Sutlers about Twenty Five Dollars for Tobacco You was in hopes that I could save enough money to buy a team but you think it is plaid out Probably it is but you do not know what I will come home with Probably that money would have it to loose you say that you have taken more than one big Cry over that money and how many more times you will have to Cry you can not tell. I think as you do that it is of no use to Cry about it now. Well we need every cent of the money that I earn, It seems hard for a Soldier to loose about Eight months and half of pay You want me to believe that you think I am not dishonest although it is a mistry to you how such a mistake was maid We are all liable to mistakes. You say that the package was not opened. That you was the one that opened it and the money was counted in the presence of three men Well that is all right Well Jane I think that I can prove it to you by the Envelope that it was opened before Father or you had possession of it. In the first place I had about

Seven or Eight Hundred Dollars to Express to different places and the Express agent had more than he could do and he gave me a pen and ink and asked me to direct the packages He said that it would help him along I done so if it is that package that I backed there is two handwriting on it unless he got the Envelope open without tare in it. Henry Perin was with me he seen all this. Well I will go to the other Sheet and see what is in it. Well I marked my money and put the amount on it if Dave and Henry had marked there money I would have maid know mistake. You do not know what to do about it. You say that Father thinks it is not right that I should loose all of it, you want me to talk to them about it and want to know whether I am certain that they sent that amount I am certain that the amount of Four Hundred Dollars was put in the Envelope you think it would be fair for everyone to loose there share of the Money I think that would be right I presume. Jane I hate to loose the money as bad as you do but I cannot cry about it for it would do know good. Well it showes what the Express agent would do if he could get a chance. We have plenty of boys in our Co. that would make him pay that money if they could but get him out by himself. The boys in the Co seem to hate it as bad as I do Well I am glad that Father will not pay that money over until gets the next letter. I presume that the other boys will loose there part of that money well I presume that I could compell them to loose the part of the money I did not bind myself for the Money. Henry seen the Money counted and he did not notice the mistake. You bet I will stick up for my rights the way the money is marked I could come nigher a makeing them loose all than for them to make me loose all but I am wiling to do the fair thing Every one that has had any thing to do with me knowes it. Well Jane you want me to tell you the truth about it can you not believe the other letters that I have sent. They ware two in number. I will have to say as I did before the money was not spent or squandered. The mistake was made in counting the money and if you cannot believe this letter you need not write to me concerning the money any more. I done the best I could and I do not grumble if Martha talked so Sausy to you I donot see why you had to take it when you had possession of the money. I shall not loose any more money and trying to get that but if they are men they will loose there share Well Jane I will tell you when I handed the money to the Express Agent he counted it over. He says to me how much did you say that there was. I said Three Hundred Dollars. I said is that right and he counted it again and said it was He knew that I had made a mistake of one Hundred Dollars and I presume that he marked the envelope so that he would know it and the first opportunity took the money out. Well Jane I have informed you of every bad deed that I have done in the Army After I sent my money I had only five dollars left Well I thought that I would make a raise with that so I took a deck of Cards and run a bank that is called quick about the first day I made Sixty some odd Dollars but since that I have lost a part of that and now I have Fifty Six Dollars a coming to me It is all in our Co I presume that I will get the most of it and if I donot I have not lost anything but that is my last gambling I havent spent any of my wages for gambling and I do not expect to do so Well Jane we have to move at an early hour in the morning We go aboard of a Transport I do not know where we are going to Yours as ever Silas I Shearer to Elizabeth J. Shearer

Columbus Texas
June 26" 1865

Dear Wife I write you a fiew to let you know where we are and how I am geting a long I am well and hearty at present hopeing that these fiew lines may find all of you well and hearty Well Jane since I last wrot to you we have taken a long ride by water and train We left Mobile the morning of the 19" Inst we arrived at Galveston the 22" the weather was very warm while crossing the Gulf the water was very Smothe We had a very nice time a Crossing the Gulf. The morning of the 23" we went aboard of the River Steamer Island City and run to Harrisburg on Buffalo Bayou five miles below Houston We got there at 10 OClock in the night The next morning (the 24") we went aboard the Cars for this place the Road runs to Alleyton about three miles from where We marched the balance of the way and got to this place after Sundown This is a small town but the surrounding Country is nice. Well Jane Texas is a pretty Country Iowa cannot surpass it for beauty Corn Crops are very good here I have not seen any small grain but I seen more Cattle the day we run threw on the Cars that I ever seen before in my life. I was telling a Doctor about seeing so many Cattle He said that I had not seen any Cattle yet he said that if I would go on a piece further than I would see Cattle he said that we came to Texas in a pore time to take a fancy to the Country He says Thermoneter stood at 102 yesterday He says that it generaly stands from 90 to 95. I think myself that the weather is very warm I have taken quite aliking to Texas but it is no use of taking I cannot live at every place that I like Well I presume that you would like to know what we came here for. I presume we came to parole the Reb Soldiers and to receive the Arms and Government property Our Regt is here a lone No Troops this side of Houston at present but our Regt There is some bushwhackers or Robers as you are pleased to Call them There is home guards in this part of the Country to protect themselves against such. There is a great many hot headed men in Texas but I think time will bring them all right They are in for Law and Order The majority of the people in Texas think our men are gentlemen to there soldiers. Well Jane I cannot tell where we will go from here probably the next time that you hear from me we will be in Mexico I was surprised when we Ordered here and now I cannot tell where we will go Well Jane it is warm and the maile is going out soon so I will close for this time I will write again soon if we do not move

Your Affectionate Husband Silas I Shearer to Elizabeth J. Shearer
(Columbus is on the West Bank of the Colorado River)
Silas I. Shearer

Wapello Co. Iowa
July 1st 1865

Dear Daughter

I received your kind letter yesterday which I was glad to read and to hear that you was all well Yours found me and Family all well and I trust this may find you well. We have a great deal of rain here for the last two or three weeks so that Farmers cannot farm and do so much. Elias has got well and has done two days work since he came home. He is getting Stout fast. We are talking some of comeing up this Fall That is if we can get off Elias talks of going this Fall and I am going along if I can. Henry Pery is going to School. The School Miss says he is a good boy. I have my Wool carded and have got my rolls at home ready for spinning. I had Seven Dozen spun and have 28 pounds more to spin. I was sorry to hear that Silas had to go to Texas I was in hopes that he would get to come home. I expect that the time seems long to you till he gets I am glad that his time out this Fall for I am uneasy about him. When he gets out all of my boys will be out. Crops look splendid at present. We will have good crops if it does not rain to much and nothing else interferes with it. The Neighborhood is healty at present no disease working In this part of the County. Andrew is well and hearty he is working at home this Summer. I don't know whether you know when Elias and Andrew was Captured and how long they stayed in Prison. Andrew was Captured on the 30th of July 1864 at <u>Sunim</u> Ga and was Prisnor 9 Months lacking two days. He was exchanged at Jacksonville, Fla on the 28th of April 1865. Elias was captured on the 13th of October at Tilton, GA and was prisonor till exchanged at Jacksonville, Fla at the same time Andrew was. I am in hopes that the Smallpox will come no nearer you than what it is. I have been looking for your Babys picture but have not got it yet. So no more I remain your Mother as every Catherine Shearer to Elizabeth Jane Shearer.

Columbus Texas
July 8th 1865

Dear Jane it has been sometime since I have written to you. today being Sunday and probably the Cars will be in tomorrow Evening if the Cars gets in we will have a chance to send our letters out it has been about Two Weeks since we have had any chance to Send letters North on the account of the R. R. Bridge across the Brazos River the water raised very Sudent and destroid the Bridge and the Cars has not been here for sometime. I am well and hearty at present and I hope that these fiew lines may find all of you well and hearty Well Jane I got a letter from Elias and Andrew they ware at home when the wrote Andrew had got his discharge but Elias was at home Sick and not discharged but he thought that he would get his discharge as soon as he was able to go to Davenport Well the boys have beat me out of the service and I am glad of it for they have seen harder times than I have. Well I cannot see as there is any prospect of us a geting out of the Service untill our time is out and that is about Seventy days then as Coln" Glasgow said to me at Mobile we will know the reason if we donot go home. probably we will stay here five or Six weeks I want to stay untill we get ready to go home and when we start so we can go with out stoping. Coln Glasgow is a Brevett Brig" Gen" the last I heard from him he was at Galveston. I understand that he is Provost Marshal Gen" of the State of Texas Well Jane about two thirds of the citizens of Texas deserves hanging they do not nor never did regard Law they was geting very bold and Saucy in this place When we came here the Major was in Command of the Regt when we got here he took Command of the Post and he put in one of those Chicago Copperheads as Provost Marshall (he is a Capt of our Regt) Well the Maj is not very Strict and the Provo Marshall run the Machien himself. The Citizens soon found that they would not be punished for these Misdemeanors so that got very Saucy drawing there revolvers on the Soldiers and threatened to Shoot them and the head men of the Regt would let it pass it was a raising the boys they would not Stand it much longer. fortunately the Lieut Coln" came the 4th Inst" he straitened things out he had not been here long before he made one Citizen pay Ten Dollars for useing about four words againste a Soldier and he has told the Provost Marshall not to let them off less than $25 Dollars for such language he has got a great many of them in Jail for the Misdemeanor towards soldiers he says he will let them know that they are a fooling with U. S. Troops and if they donot behave themselves he will fill the jail full of them those men that are so mean are men that was in the rear or at home and they are a blowing what they can do and that they have not been whiped but when one of the Soldiers comes down on them they are not so brave if they could slip up and Shoot a person probably they would do it Confederate Soldiers that was in the Ranks and done there duty dispise such men as bad as we do and say if they had been to the front where the Soldiers had been that they would have been whiped those men that want good Laws say such hot headed men Should be hanged up to a tree That is my Sentiments The boys upholds Coln" Clark in his Strict Orders the Town is geting very peaceful the boys donot like to have a fuss with the Citizens They look to the authorities to tend to such business but if Coln Clark had not come I presume that we would have had a big muss here The boys will not hurt good loyal men Well Jane we are blessed with Negroes here they are badly used by there Masters I have heard of several being shot by the overseeres and that is a very poor way to get any thing to like them. those men that have gave there Negroes there freedom and have used them right they will not leave them they stay and work for them and get paid I have seen some Negros here that I would liked to tied a rope around there necks and tied them up to a lim. I know you donot like Negros there for I will not say any more about them. your affectionate Husband

S. I. Shearer to E. P. Shearer

Vicksburg
July the 26th 1865

Beloved Companion It is once more that I write you a fiew lines to inform you of my health which is not very good at present but not dangerous I am so as I can go around I hope these lines will find you all well and enjoying pleasure I walked about a quarter of a mile yesterday to where the Regt was and I received two letters from you I received one from you two or three weeks ago and I was very glad to hear from you that you ware all well I like to hear such news it is the best news that I can hear you write to me that you would send the children likeness if I wanted them I would like to see them very much but I guess you had better not send them for I have no way of taken care of them I must tell you where I am I am on the Nashville Hospital Boat I do not know how long I will remain on it whether I will be sent up the River or not the sick are all being sent up the River as fast as possible. There is some talk of our Regt going up the River and if they do I will try and go with them for I would like to go North I would come home on a furloug if I could get the chance but I expect the chance would be pretty slim for me at present and it would cost three or four months wages to get from here to home and back out I think probably I would get my health if I was in the North I know I would rather be in the North than in the Sunny South as they call it I am in hopes our men will keep gaining ground untill the Rebellion will play out and then we can all return home and live in peace once more There is a great many sick soldiers here at Vicksburg and it is hard that they cant bee sent home where they can be taken care of I seen Lias and Barty a fiew days ago Lias was well and hearty Barty he was sick I have not heard how he is geting a long You must excuse me for writing with a pencil for I have no ink Soldiers has to do as they can not as they wisht I understood they was a Show at Newton and they had two or three whit Negroes in it If they folks would come down here they could se a great many white Negoes I suppose you know what I mean (It is Soldiers) Direct your letters to the Regt untill further orders So no more at present from you affectionate

Husband Silas I Shearer to E. J. Shearer

I would like to see you all.

Probably written August 1865
Monday 10th

Well Jane the Mail goes out today at One OClock I will write a fiew more lines the Caro Came in last night I presume there was know mail for us this time I havenot heard of any as yet. Although I would be very much pleased to get a letter from home but I will have to content myself without one. It has been so long since I have writen to you that you may think that we are out of the United States but I have to write as I can. Our Regt has considerable of work to do before we leave here. One Hundred Miles Square is aloted to this Regt the Parole and the Ammesty Oath is given to Every person within this line. And all of the Reble Government property has to be brough in an turned over to the Authorities of the United States and it will take some time to do all of this I think by the time that all of this work is done it will be between the 10th of August and the 1st of September if such is the case we probably will get home about the 18th of September perhaps it will be in October. it is very easy to get in the Service but it is a dificult mater to get out. I wanted to get home so I could make some hay for myself but that question is decided now if I can I want to buy some calves this fall and I will want some hay I want you to get me some hay cut if you can and have it stacked at the North side of my Stable if it does not cost too much to have it Stacked there I donot want you to wait for me to come home to make hay for I cannot be there in time. I thought a while last Spring that I would be at home for the fourth of July but I took the fourth of July in Camp at Columbus and I have a piece of roast turkey. Well Jane I was to Church up town one week ago last night. I seen Several ladies there. that was the first Singing that I have heard ladies do since I left home. I am a shamed to tell it but this was the first meeting I have been to Since we left Oald Town Texas I must close Youres as ever

Silas I Shearer

Quotes from Allen's History of Story County

At a meeting of the farmers of Story County held at the Courthouse in Nevada on September 17, 1881. It was agreed to organize a Farmer's Protective Association subject to the Constitution and By-Laws of the State Association of Iowa. C. P. McCord was chosen Chairman and A. M. Norris, Secretary. S. I. Shearer, Collins Center, enrolled as a member.

Silas I. Shearer was known as one who raises stock for sale and is a citizen of some energy.

Silas I. Shearer served the Story County Board of Supervisors from 1875 through 1878. While on the Board he supervised the construction of the Courthouse which was constructed in 1877, designed by William Foster, and erected at a cost of $40,000.00.

Old Settlers of the County settled prior to January 1, 1858. Silas I. Shearer, Elias W. Shearer, and Benjamin Shenkle.

OBITUARY OF SILAS SHEARER
"Another Pioneer Departed"

Silas I. Shearer was born in Marion County, Indiana, January 11, 1838 and died in Collins, Iowa on March 5, 1915, having lived 77 years, 1 month and 25 days.

Mr. Shearer came with his parents to Wapello County, Iowa, September 30, 1847. He remained in Wapello County until he was a young man, then he went to Des Moines, in 1856, when that city was a small place. In November 1856 he came to Nevada and lodged in the old log hotel, "Old Terrific." The next day he walked to the lower part of the County, now known as Collins Township. He spent 3 years in Missouri and lived in Iowa about 65 years. He served Collins Township several times as Justice of the Peace, also as member of the Board of Supervisors and was acting as such when the present courthouse was built.

In August 1862 Mr. Shearer enlisted in Co. K, 23rd Iowa Volunteers. He was promoted to Sergeant June 1, 1865. He was mustered out at the close of the War. His regiment numbered 1070 in the beginning and had 316 mustered out, having engaged in many battles.

Mr. Shearer was united in marriage to Miss Elizabeth Shenkle, November 30, 1859. To this happy union were born 11 children, two of whom have preceded father and mother to the other world. Mrs. Shearer left her husband just one year and two weeks before his death. Mr. Shearer was heard to say that he would not live more than a year alone. There are 9 children, 46 grandchildren, 7 great grandchildren, three brothers, one sister and a great number of friends who mourn the loss of a loving father, a sincere friend, a noble citizen.

Mr. Shearer united with the Evangelical Church at old West Point school house in 1871. After moving to Bondurant, he with his wife, united with the Congregational Church, in which his membership was enjoyed till death translated name to book of eternal life. His old comrades, his loving and large family of children and his many friends will have many kind and sweet memories to cherish of this deal old gentleman in the future.

The funeral was held in the M. P. Church Sunday afternoon. The church was filled, relatives and friends, being present to show their respect for the deceased and give mutual sympathy. The music was furnished by an efficient choir of voices, who sang appropriate selections. The floral tributes were very beautiful. Rev. C. S. Hanson conducted the service and preached the sermon, which was replete with tender, comforting thoughts, appreciative of the noble earthly life that had just closed and giving Christian assurance for the life eternal. Rev. A. V. Hart read the scripture lesson and Rev. Lyle offered prayer.

The children with their families who mourn the loss of an earthly father are Lewis D. Shearer of Collins, Eliza E. Bence of State Center, Sanford A. Shearer of Gilbert, Minnie M. Kimberley of Collins, Ora B. Heintz of State Center, Catherine L. Diggins of Collins, Elias W. Shearer of Colo, Hattie S. Girton of Ardmore, S. Dakota. These sorrowing children have the sympathy of all their many friends. All were present except James G. who was snowbound.

The pallbearers were six grandsons: Frank Kimberley, Oliver Shearer, Lewis Bence, Isaiah Kimberley, Sanford Shearer, Jr., and Fred Bence. The interment was in Collins Cemetery. They were the same pallbearers as served at the funeral of Grandmother Shearer.

The following relatives and friends were in attendance from out-of-town. Mr. and Mrs. Sanford Shearer and son Igo of Gilbert and sons Roy of Perry and Marshall of Des Moines. Mr. and Mrs. Lewis Bence of State Center, Mr. and Mrs. W. C. Heintz of State Center, Mr. and Mrs. A. L. Girton of Ardmore, S. Dakota, Mr. and Mrs. M. M. Shearer of Colo, Iowa, George Shearer of Tama, Mrs. J. L. Shearer of Rhodes, Mrs. Melissa Reicks and daughter Letta of Bondurant, Mr. and Mrs. E. W. Shearer of Colo